Anna Doyle Miller
D0209322

THE LION

THE

LION

BY

Joseph Kessel

TRANSLATED FROM THE FRENCH BY

PETER GREEN

NEW YORK ALFRED A KNOPF *1959*

L. C. CATALOG CARD NUMBER: 59–10061

© ALFRED A. KNOPF, INC., 1959

❧ THIS IS A BORZOI BOOK,
PUBLISHED BY ALFRED A. KNOPF, INC. ❧

Originally published in French as LE LION. © 1958, Librairie Gallimard.

PART ONE

Had he pulled at my eyelids

to find out what they concealed? I couldn't be certain about this. As I woke up I had the distinct impression that something like a coarse paintbrush was being drawn lightly across my face. But when I became fully conscious I saw that he was sitting on the pillow beside me, and staring at me with concentrated absorption.

He was scarcely bigger than a full-sized coconut, and his short fur was much the same color. It made him look like a children's toy: he was furry all over except for his face, which resembled a black silk domino. Through this mask gleamed two bright and liquid eyes.

Dawn had just broken, but I had been so tired the night before that I had forgotten to put out my hurricane lamp. Accordingly my extraordinary morning visitor showed up in clear silhouette against the whitewashed roughcast of the wall. A few hours later I should have taken his appearance for granted. His tribe had their headquarters in the tall trees scattered round my bungalow; whole families of relatives crowded on every branch. But I had only arrived, worn out, the previous evening, after nightfall.

◇◇

That was why I now held my breath and stared at the tiny monkey crouching so close to my face.

He kept as still as I did. Even his eyes, like drops of clear dark water in that silky black mask, remained fixed, unwinking. His expression was utterly devoid of either fear, distrust, or, indeed, mere curiosity. I was simply an object for calm and serious contemplation.

Then his furry little head—no bigger than the clenched fist of a newborn baby—bent a little to one side. The wise eyes looked sad and full of pity. He was sorry for me. He seemed to want to give me some kind of advice or warning: what, I could not tell. But I felt he was friendly.

I must have made some slight movement without being aware of it. The coppery ball of fur, all shot through with smoke-dark undertones, bounded away from bed to chair to table, and so out by the open window, where it vanished in the morning mist.

My bush shirt and drill trousers were lying on the ground at the foot of the camp bed, beside the hurricane lamp, just as I had thrown them down before retiring. I put them on and went out onto the veranda.

The previous evening, I recalled, I had observed—despite the darkness—that my bungalow was surrounded on three sides by dense thorny scrub. Out in front a huge clearing stretched away into the night. But this morning everything was hidden by mist. There was only one landmark visible. Away on the horizon, directly facing me, on the very edge of the world, towered the gigantic peak of Kilimanjaro, sheathed in its eternal snows.

A noise rather like someone, very furtively, shaking dice in a box drew my attention to the bare wooden steps that led up to the veranda. Slowly, but with deliberate purpose-fulness, a gazelle was climbing them. There was no mistaking it; this *was* a gazelle, though so tiny a specimen that its ears hardly reached my knees. Its horns were no bigger than pine needles, and its hooves about the size of a man's thumbnail.

This extraordinary creature, having materialized out of the mist, never stopped till it reached my ankles. Then it lifted its muzzle and looked at me. I stooped down, taking great care not to alarm it, and stretched out one hand to stroke that fine-drawn, exquisitely proportioned head. The little gazelle stood its ground. Gently I caressed its nostrils, and it did not shrink from my touch. Its eyes met mine: there was an extraordinary gentleness apparent in them which seemed to me somehow identical with the little monkey's expression of melancholy wisdom. Once more I failed to understand the message that was being given me.

As though apologizing for its inability to speak, the gazelle licked my fingers. Then, very softly, it drew away from me. Once more its hooves clicked on the steps like small rattling dice, and then it was gone, and I was alone once more. But already, during that brief interlude, the tropical dawn—an amazingly short-lived phenomenon—had passed into morning. Out of the heart of darkness light suddenly sprang, gloriously arrayed, darting shafts of splendor. The whole world broke into brilliant, sparkling iridescence: crimson arrows streaked across the snows of Kilimanjaro.

The sunlight melted the mist away, breaking it up into tattered wisps and wreaths and spirals of steamy air which, in their turn, condensed into heavy dew, all spangled and twinkling like crushed diamonds. The grass, normally so parched and yellow, now for a moment shone in dewy magnificence.

From the treetops round my bungalow, where spiky thorns glinted fresh in the morning air, came a chorus of bird song and simian chattering. In front of my veranda, layer after layer of floating mist shredded away to reveal a rich green glade, which grew both in depth and mystery as each dissolving patch of vapor revealed yet more mist beyond.

The earth was like a stage at the beginning of some theatrical performance: one by one the curtains were rising to present another day in the world's endless drama.

Finally, while a faint haze still hung in the air, at the far end of the clearing a shimmer of water showed through. It did not fit exactly into any category: it was neither lake, pool, nor swamp. Fed doubtless by some tiny underground spring, it shivered in rippling equipoise among the tall grasses, reeds, and tangled scrub: a shallow liquid skin of water that lacked the strength to spread any farther.

At the edge of the water were the wild animals.

I had seen them often enough, from road or track, during the journey I had just made through East Africa, in Kenya, Uganda, Tanganyika and elsewhere. But on such occasions I got no more than vague, fleeting glimpses of herds that scattered at the sound of our approaching car, terrified shadows seen for an instant and then gone. When, as sometimes happened, I got the chance to observe a wild beast without his knowledge, it was always done either from a considerable distance or by use of a "hide." In both cases I felt I was cheating.

The spectacle of these free, innocent creatures going about their business in the parched bush had an extraordinary effect on me. I watched them with a mixture of eagerness, exaltation, jealousy, and despair. I felt as though I had rediscovered a paradise known or dreamed of in some long-forgotten age. I had found my way back to the very threshold of this Elysium, yet could not cross it.

On each successive occasion, as the edge of my frustration grew keener, I found myself driven by a steadily increasing need—childish, no doubt, but incontrovertible— to win admittance to the fresh, innocent atmosphere of the primeval world. I made up my mind that, before returning to Europe, I would visit one of the National Parks in Kenya, where rigorously enforced game laws ensure the protection of every kind of wild life.

Now that wild life stood before me.

The animals were no longer suspicious, on the alert, or driven by self-protective fear to band themselves together according to species in herds, bevies, troops, or packs. The water's edge was neutral territory; here they met and mingled with superbly relaxed confidence, at peace with the bush, the morning air, and each other.

I was too far away from them to study their movements or beautifully blending colors in any detail; but close enough to see that they had gathered in their hundreds, every sort together, and that this moment of their lives was utterly devoid of fear or hatred. Gazelles, antelopes, giraffes, gnus, zebras, rhinos, buffalo, elephants—the animals came and went at a leisurely pace, casually, as and when their thirst dictated.

The rays of the sun, still mild and new-risen, shone

slanting across the snow slopes that crowned Kilimanjaro. A cool morning breeze was blowing away the last wisps of mist. Pools and feeding-grounds appeared through a fine gauze-like haze, with their complement of muzzles and snouts, bodies dark, dappled or striped, trunks and tusks, and every variety of horn—straight, curved, thick, thin, blunt, or pointed. Together they made up a fantastic tapestry, all hung from the highest mountain in Africa.

I cannot recall how and when I walked down the veranda steps toward them. I no longer had any control over my movements. I felt these wild creatures drawing me on to find a primal happiness older than mankind itself. I took the path that ran along the side of the clearing, backed by a curtain of trees and bushes. By coming closer to this magic scene I did not destroy it; on the contrary, it acquired richer substance and solidity. With every step I took it became easier to distinguish the various species, to appreciate their strength or gracefulness. I saw the sheen of the antelopes' coats, the terrible ridged forehead of the buffalo, the granite-like texture of the elephant's skin.

They all went on cropping the grass, lapping at the water's edge, or wandering from one tuft or puddle to the next, undisturbed by my approach. They were *there*, in their own domain, peaceful and contented. Each step I took made them a little more real, a little less inaccessible.

By now I had reached the edge of the scrub. It only remained to break cover, to step out on that damp, gleaming ground beside the watering-place in order to experience the friendship and acceptance of the wild creatures in their own private territory. Nothing could hold me back any longer. Common sense and the instinct for self-preservation were ousted by another urge, as powerful as it was obscure, that drove me forward in the direction of this other, alien world. At long last my desire was to be satisfied.

But, precisely at this moment, a warning signal flashed in my brain, pulling me up short. I sensed a presence near me, opposing my purpose, exerting its will against mine. It was certainly not an animal: I had already gone over to the animals' side, and belonged to their world. The creature whose nearness I had, by some unanalyzable sixth sense, contrived to divine was beyond doubt human.

Then a voice said, in English: "You must not go any farther."

I looked, and saw a slight figure hardly more than a yard away from me, standing in the shadow of a giant wait-a-bit thorn tree. There was no attempt at concealment; but absolute immobility combined with a set of gray overalls made this person appear to be part of the tree trunk against which they rested.

It was, I realized, a child of about twelve, with a dark fringe and a bowl-shaped haircut. His face was round, and his smooth skin tanned a deep brown. He had a long, slender neck. His large brown eyes hardly seemed to notice me at all; they were fixed unwinkingly on the animals. I felt annoyed and embarrassed: I had been caught by a child behaving in an ultra-childish fashion myself.

In a low voice I whispered: "Can't people go down to the lake? Is it out of bounds?"

There was a brief nod of the cropped head, but the child's eyes still followed every movement of the animals.

"Are you quite sure?" I persisted.

"Who should know better than me?" the child re-marked. "My father is the Warden of this Reserve."

"Ah, I understand," I said. "He's made his son responsi-ble for looking after it."

At last the large brown eyes looked directly at me. For the first time that small, tanned face took on an expres-sion appropriate to its age.

"You're wrong," said the child in gray overalls. "I'm not a boy, I'm a girl; and my name is Patricia."

2

It was not the first time—as her mischievously trium-phant expression made quite plain—that Patricia had sprung this particular surprise on a visitor. At the same time, doubtless to make her declaration more convincing, she subtly altered her whole appearance: smile, stance, even the poise of her neck now quickened into seduc-tively feminine warmth. It was a naïve yet timeless ges-ture, which gave the childish figure, at last, its full, per-sonal identity.

I probably needed a shock of this sort to bring me back to some awareness of real life. Here was a little girl, soon after sunrise, all alone in the bush, within a stone's throw of numerous wild beasts.

"Do they let you go out so early, so far away from the house?" I asked her.

Patricia made no reply. Her features had frozen into a grave immobility again; once more her face might have been that of a boy. She was staring at the wild game as though I didn't exist.

The light was now streaming up, warm and shimmering, from the deep springs of the dawn. The water sparkled as the sun caught it, and the animals crowded round its brink took on a fresh dimension of solidity.

The urge which had driven me to this point now flooded back in full force. No little girl was going to balk me of my satisfaction at the last moment. I took a step forward toward the clearing.

Patricia did not bother to turn her head; she merely repeated: "Don't go there."

"I suppose you'll tell your father, and he'll turn me off the Reserve?" I inquired.

"I'm not a tell-tale," Patricia said, staring at me defiantly. Her child's sense of honor shone out of her eyes, naked and appealing.

"Are you afraid something might happen to me, then?" I persisted.

"You're big enough to look after yourself," Patricia said. "And anyway, I couldn't care less what happens to you."

How could this fresh, innocent young creature suddenly have such a change of mood? What could make her indifferent to the point of positive cruelty? The violence I might suffer from the hooves and claws and horns of angry wild beasts was supremely unimportant to her. She would have watched me trampled or gored to death without turning a hair.

"But—but—" I stammered, "in that case, why do you ask me not to—"

"It's perfectly simple," snapped Patricia. My slowness

was beginning to irritate her. Sparks of anger flashed in her big dark eyes.

"Surely you can see how peaceful and at ease all these animals are with one another," she went on. "This is the best part of their day."

It may have been due to the early hour, or the exotic setting, but a most extraordinary power seemed to emanate from this young girl. At moments she appeared both to possess a certainty of judgment entirely unrelated to her years, and to understand a kind of truth far removed from rational cognition. It was as though she had her being outside, indeed *beyond* the normal human pattern.

"I have no wish to disturb the animals," I told her. "All I want is to live for a little while in their company, to share their existence."

Patricia gave me a searching, suspicious look.

"Do you *really* love them?" she demanded.

"I think I do," I said.

Her huge, somber eyes remained fixed in thought for a while. Then a trusting smile lit up every feature of that infinitely sensitive face.

"I think so too," she said.

I find it hard to express the joy I felt at this smile and the words which followed it.

"Then you will let me go on?" I said.

"No." Patricia's refusal was confirmed by a gentle, but inexorable, shake of the cropped head on its long, delicate neck.

"Why?"

Patricia did not answer at once. She continued to look at me, silent and pensive: indeed, there was much friendliness about her expression. But it was a special sort of

friendliness: disinterested, serious, melancholy, pitying
—and powerless to help.

Somewhere I had already seen this strange expression.
But where? Then I remembered the little monkey and the
miniature gazelle that had visited me in my bungalow. In
Patricia's eyes I rediscovered that mysterious sadness
peculiar to the animal kingdom. But there was one great
difference: the child, unlike the beasts, could talk.

At last Patricia said: "The animals want no part of you.
They can't enjoy real peace and freedom when you're near
them. That's what they want, and that's what they normally have."

"But I love them," I said. "You believe that yourself—"

"It makes no difference. The animals are not for you.
You have to possess that special knowledge to qualify. It's
not in you. You could never learn it."

She fumbled momentarily for a phrase which would
make her meaning clearer. Then she gave a faint shrug
of her thin shoulders, and said: "You come from too far
away. And anyway it's too late." She leaned back more
heavily against the big thorn tree. Her gray, neutral
clothes made her look a part of it.

Every minute the sunlight came streaming more
strongly through the tangled thickets of the bush. The
undergrowth was transformed into fine golden tracery,
while from every hidden lair fresh wild families appeared,
making for the water and the lush grass. To avoid disturb-
ing earlier arrivals, these latecomers skirted the outer
edges of the clearing: some actually passed by the belt of
scrub behind which Patricia and I were standing. But
even these I now knew to be *tabu* as far as I was concerned, more inaccessible than if their grazing-ground

had been those ageless snowfields that crowned Kilimanjaro, and which gleamed at me from the end of the world,
the farthest limits of the morning sky.

"Too far away," the child had said; "too late." There was
nothing I could set against her absolute certainty: when
she spoke those words her eyes were as gentle as the
little gazelle's, as wise as the little monkey's.

Suddenly I felt the touch of Patricia's hand on mine,
and could not repress a start of surprise. Not a sound, not
even the snap of a twig, had forewarned me of her movement toward me. The top of her head only came up to my
elbow; and her body, compared to mine, was extraordinarily frail and puny. Yet I felt, in those rough, chapped
little fingers that now grasped my hand, the desire to offer protection, consolation even. Then, as one might ad-
dress a child who has just obeyed an unpleasant command, and attempt to compensate it for its unhappiness,
Patricia said: "Perhaps I'll take you to another place later.
You'll see everything you want there, I promise you."

It was only then that I noticed Patricia's curious manner of speech. Up till this moment her personality and
behavior had more or less hypnotized me. But now I observed that this little girl used her voice as people do
whose conversation must not be overheard: prisoners,
patrol-leaders, hunters and trappers. It was a secret, neutral voice, totally devoid of all vibrancy, resonance or
timbre: somehow it conveyed a quality of silence. It occurred to me that, quite unconsciously, I had been copy-
ing Patricia's clipped verbal economy.

I said: "It's not hard to believe that even the most savage beast might accept you as a friend."

The childish fingers resting on mine trembled with

sheer joy. Patricia's hand was suddenly the hand of a happy little girl, and no more. The face turned toward mine, in a quiet ecstasy of delight; the great dark eyes were suddenly lit and sparkling and expressed simply the pleasure of a child who has heard the words best calculated to please it.

"You know," Patricia said—and despite the emotion which sent the blood pulsing through her tanned cheeks, her voice remained as flat and secretive as ever—"you know, my father swears I understand wild animals better than he does. And make no mistake about it, my father has spent his whole life among them. He knows them all—in Kenya, Uganda, Tanganyika, the Rhodesias, everywhere. But with me it's different, he says. *Different.*"

Patricia tossed her head, and the close-cropped fringe lifted a little to reveal a surprisingly white and delicate forehead. Her glance fell on my hand, and on her own small paw, nails broken and lined with dirt, which now reposed in it.

"You're not a hunter," she said.

"Quite right. How did you know, though?"

Patricia laughed silently. "No one can hide anything from me here."

"All the same," I said, "no one's spoken to me yet. No one's even seen me."

"*No one?* What about Thauku, the reception clerk, who entered your name in the book yesterday evening? And Matcha, the boy who carried your luggage, and Awori, the sweeper responsible for your bungalow?"

"These blacks can know nothing of what I do or don't do," I said.

An expression of childish mischievousness flashed

across Patricia's face: the same expression that accompanied her earlier remark about being a girl, not a boy.

"I suppose you haven't thought of your driver," she said.

"What—*Bogo?*"

"He knows you very well indeed," Patricia said. "Two months ago you hired a car in Nairobi, and he's driven you everywhere since then."

"Bogo couldn't tell you much. I've never met a more taciturn, laconic character in my life."

"When he speaks English, perhaps," Patricia said.

"You mean to say you—"

"Of course. I know Kikuyu as well as he does. When I was a baby my first nurse was a Kikuyu. I speak Swahili too, because every native tribe understands it. I speak Wakamba because my father's favorite tracker is a Wakamba, and Masai because the Masai have camping rights in the Reserve, and can pass through it at will."

Patricia was still smiling, but her smile no longer merely mocked me with conscious superiority. It once more reflected both her calm self-assurance and that faculty she possessed for communicating with the most primitive creatures according to the laws of their own private universe.

"The natives of this district come and tell me everything," Patricia went on. "I know far more about their affairs than even my father does. He only knows Swahili—and besides, he pronounces even that like a European. Anyway, he's a disciplinarian—in his job he has to be. But I never tell tales to him. All our employees—houseboys, guards, and all—know that, so they're willing to talk to me. Thauku, the clerk, told me that you had a

French passport and lived in Paris. The boy who carried your bags told me you had a heavy caseful of books. The sweeper said that the white man wouldn't let him heat any water for a bath, and was so tired that he went to bed without eating a thing."

"Yes," I said, "and I'd be sleeping still if I hadn't been waked up by a very early caller. Still, I have no doubt *he* came and reported to you as well." And I told Patricia about the tiny monkey and the gazelle.

"Oh, yes," she said. "That was Nicholas and Cymbeline." Her expression as she spoke of them was affectionate, but faintly contemptuous. "They're my pets. But they let anyone stroke them, just as though they were cats or dogs."

"Oh," I said. "Really?"

Patricia could hardly realize how she had hurt me by reducing my two mysterious dawn messengers to the banal status of mere pets.

"Out there," Patricia said, "it's a different matter entirely." She pointed toward the grazing-ground and the water hole, crowded now with wild game, the great snowclad, cloudy mountain looming above them in the background. Her hand trembled as she spoke; and even her voice abandoned its usual easy toneless neutrality and now carried an edge of real feeling. Yet even so this feeling remained a suggestion only; her emotions were not fully released.

She said: "These creatures belong to no one. They have no notion of what obedience means. Even if they accept you, they still preserve their independence. If you want to join their play, you have to understand all kinds of weather lore, for a start. You must know every inch of their grazing-grounds. You have to know the taste of every plant they eat, and be able to tell good water from bad. And you must instinctively guess their mood—and watch out when they're mating or have young cubs. You must run and breathe as they do, share their amusements, even imitate their characteristic silences."

"Did your father teach you all this?" I asked.

"My father doesn't know half as much as I do," Patricia said. "He hasn't the time. He's too old now. No, I learned it all by myself, on my own."

She suddenly looked up at me; and on that proud, stubborn, brown little face I now observed a most improbable expression—one, indeed, of which I should hardly have thought her capable. She looked hesitant, almost humble.

"Are you sure—I mean, please tell me the truth—are you *really* sure I won't bore you if I go on talking about wild animals?" she blurted out. Then, observing my astonishment, she quickly added: "My mother always tells me that grownups couldn't possibly take any interest in my stories."

I said: "I could gladly spend the whole day listening to them."

"You mean it," she gasped. "You really mean it!"

Patricia's strange excitement surprised and slightly worried me. She grasped my hand with sudden eagerness: her fingers had become burning hot, and her jagged, broken nails dug into my skin. Such symptoms, I reflected, signified something more than the mere pleasure of satisfying a childish longing. They showed a deep, frustrated need; and Patricia clearly took this frustration very badly. Was it possible that already she had to pay a price for her dreams and her peculiar powers—the price of loneliness?

She began to talk again; and though her voice remained muted and oddly without modulation—perhaps, indeed, because of this quality—she sounded like a natural echo of the thoughts of the bush itself.

Her words struck a perfect yet dynamic balance between the agonized effort which thought demands, and its impotent striving to penetrate the mystery—the only mystery worth solving—of creation and all created things. She dissolved worry and perplexity by a kind of soothing hypnotic magic. This was the magic whisper we hear when a faint breeze rustles among the wild osiers and tall bush grass: a perennial, changeless murmur. Patricia's voice had no truck now with human affairs, in all their restrictive futility. What she possessed was the gift of establishing contact and communication between man's unhappy prison of the self and that kingdom of truth, freedom, and innocence which spread and blossomed in the African dawn.

I thought of the endless treks through the Reserve, the countless vigils in dense, thorny thickets, the inexhaustible patience and mysterious instinctive sensibility which must have combined to give Patricia that depth of experience and knowledge which she was now sharing with me. These roaming herds, unapproachable by anyone else, had become her familiar friends. She knew their tribes and families: she knew each individual animal. In this closed society she had her special *entrées*, her accepted customs, and the usual quota of friends and enemies.

The buffalo we could see wallowing about in the water hole clearly had a chronically bad temper. The old elephant with worn, broken tusks enjoyed a romp as much as the youngest of his great-grandchildren; but his wife, a big, slate-gray creature, who was at the moment engaged in pushing her young down to the water with her trunk, had a sense of propriety that almost amounted to an obsession.

I studied the impalas, who bore a black arrow-like marking on each golden flank, and who were the most elegant as well as the most easily alarmed of the antelope species. Patricia pointed out the ones who let her approach them without showing fear. Then there were the tiny bush bucks, with their spiraling horns, infinitely brave for all their fragile appearance: the toughest fighters among them accepted Patricia as a friend.

Then she turned to the zebras. There was one, she told me, that she had seen escape from a bush fire. It could easily be identified by the burns and scorch marks that freckled its body between the black stripes.

She had once witnessed a rhinoceros fight: the huge male now standing a few yards away from us, horn in air, a granite chunk of prehistory, had been the victor. But the battle had left its mark on him, in the shape of a frightful scar, as deep as it was long. This scar suddenly became visible when the fluttering mass of white egrets who served him as tick-scavengers flew up off his back.

The giraffes too had their private history, as did the big hump-backed gnus, old and young, generation after generation: a chronicle of frisking pleasures, grim struggles for supremacy, the vicissitudes of migration and rutting desire. When I look back on these tales, I see that in setting them down I have—despite all my efforts not to do so—sorted them out into some sort of ordered sequence, dealt with them methodically. But Patricia contrived to talk about them all simultaneously: the conventions of logic and reason had no place in her mind. She let herself be carried away by each momentary impulse; her mental associations were primitive in the extreme, and she reacted instinctively to the guiding dictates of her senses. This, indeed, was how those beautiful, uncomplicated creatures we were watching themselves behaved. They lived untouched by human guilt or anguish simply through having no knowledge of the profitless, illusory urge which men possess to measure out time, to order the world. They lived and died without ever once needing to ask the question, "Why?"

In this way the essential nature of the animals' way of life, in all its clarity and profundity, was revealed to me, and my mind became illuminated like tangled undergrowth through which a sudden shaft of sunlight strikes. I saw the nocturnal lairs from which each of these wild creatures had been drawn at daybreak, and the hunting-grounds to which they would disperse after the dawn truce by the water was over. Now the plains and hills and jungle and bush and savannahs which made up the vast Reserve through which I had driven the day before became for me, simply, the private estates, homes, places of refuge, and native soil of every species and family I had observed. Here the impala bounded free, and herds of buffalo browsed. Here zebra and elephant roamed at their ease.

Suddenly it struck me that one clan was missing from this animal kingdom, and that the most superb of all.

"What about the great carnivores?" I asked Patricia.

This question did not surprise her in the least. I felt that she had been expecting it, and knew what I was going to say at the very instant I opened my mouth.

I felt then that we had reached a degree of understanding where the difference in our ages no longer counted. The intensity of our freely admitted common interests and needs had done the trick. With the wild animals as a connecting link, a bond of complicity and equality had been established between a young child and a man who, for a long time now, had ceased to be a man in the true sense of that word.

Patricia closed her eyes. A private smile, meant for herself alone, lit up her features with a kind of inner glow. It reminded me of the smile sometimes observable on the face of a very small child while asleep: a secret smile, its outline barely sketched, yet charged with a certain mysterious happiness. Then Patricia raised her eyelids, looked up, and let me share a part at least of this special smile. I felt she had made a promise of a sort: the moment seemed to mark a vitally important pact between us.

"I'll take you to the right place," Patricia said.

"When?"

"Don't be in such a hurry," she replied gently. "You have to be patient, always, when you're dealing with animals. You must take time."

"I know—it's just that—"

I couldn't get the sentence out. Patricia's hand, which all this time had rested trustingly in mine, was suddenly pulled away in a sharp, abrupt movement. Her big dark eyes in an instant went blank, lost all their expressiveness. Something resembling a premature wrinkle appeared between them.

"You're only staying here a very short time, aren't you?" she said. She was looking at me in so odd a way that I couldn't bring myself to give her a straight answer.

"I don't really know," I stammered.

"That's a lie. You know perfectly well. You told the reception clerk that you were leaving the Reserve tomorrow." The line between her eyebrows deepened. "I'd forgotten that," she whispered. Her lips were compressed tightly together, but even so she could not stop them trembling entirely. It hurt me to see her like this.

"I must apologize for wasting your valuable time," she said, and turned away to study the grazing animals.

I said, clumsily: "Even if I do go away, we're friends now."

Patricia swung round to face me, in a single violent— yet soundless—movement.

"I have no friends," she said. "You're just like the rest of them."

The rest of them: casual tourists, idly curious or indifferent. People from big, far-off cities who drove through in their cars, leaned out of the window to get a fleeting glimpse of *la vie sauvage,* and went on their way again.

I seemed to see the dead sea of loneliness closing its waters once more above the child's head.

"I have no friends," Patricia repeated.

She walked away from me, out of the cover of the scrub, into the clearing. Not so much as a twig cracked underfoot as she went. Her shoulders were hunched forward, and her head was sunk into them. Then the tiny gray figure, with its bowl-shaped haircut, passed into the shimmering tapestry of wild life at the foot of Kilimanjaro, and became a part of it.

3

I felt so savage a stab of utter loneliness that, at its first onslaught, I refused to believe that such agony could be true. It was absurd, out of all proportion. It couldn't have any substantial existence, much less a real meaning. I possessed numerous friends—faithful, reliable, chosen and tried in the course of a long life. Soon I would return home and tell them about my African trip. They, in their turn, would tell me everything, good or bad, that had happened to them in my absence. My house was waiting for me—built to my own specifications and full of familiar, comforting objects. Lastly, there was my work: a sufficient world in itself to contain me.

But it was in vain that I counted up my blessings, and tried to justify my existence in the light of sweet reason. Nothing could replace the wonderful sense of fullness and completion I had experienced a few moments before, when the occupants of the clearing still seemed to accept me among them. Now I was alone: lost, abandoned, rejected, without hope or purpose till the day I died.

Patricia had left me with her own agony, and had gone to join the beasts.

I ought to follow her, I told myself. Someone has to protect her. But I did not even make an attempt to do so. At one stroke I had become aware once more of my age. I felt the weight and bulk of my body, observed my own clumsy movements—all inescapably branding me as the product of human civilization. I began to think again.

The idea of "protecting" Patricia was, of course, ridiculous. I was proposing to plunge in among those tall grasses and primeval waters, where a light-footed, silent, quick-moving fauna, their tempers as fierce as their senses were acute, would hem me in on all sides—and why? To follow a little girl who would vanish among the beasts of the bush like a naiad plunging into a pool, or an elf scuttling away in the forest. It was really high time I came back to earth.

The Warden of the Reserve, the master and guardian of every wild animal it contained, was Patricia's father. It was his business to assume responsibility for his daughter's waking dreams. I was a stranger, a casual visitor; it was no affair of mine.

I turned my back on the clearing and made my way to the compound reserved for guests visiting the National Park.

It had been planned in such a way as not to alter the natural landscape, and consisted of about a dozen "bungalows" half-hidden by tall trees. These "bungalows" were really round, native-style huts: with their mud walls, finished in roughcast lime, and their pointed thatch roofs, they looked like any of the local villages.

The place was empty: this was not the tourist season. Besides, Kenya was at the time in the throes of Mau Mau terrorism. When I got back to the bungalow that I had chosen at random the night before, the little monkey was waiting for me on the veranda. His eyes, as wise and melancholy as ever, gazed at me through their silky black domino. He seemed to be saying: Well, I warned you, didn't I? But this time, instead of vanishing into thin air, as he had done at daybreak, he jumped up on my shoulder.

I recalled the name that Patricia had referred to him by, and said, softly: "Nicholas! Hey, Nicholas!"

He gently scratched the back of my neck. I offered him my hand, palm uppermost, and he squatted comfortably in it. He weighed no more than a big ball of wool; I enjoyed stroking his short fur. But an animal that could so quickly be won over to such an extent was no more than a pleasant cellmate for Man in his unbreakable prison.

I put Nicholas down on the balustrade that ran along the veranda, and glanced, despite myself, in the direction of the clearing. There, too, the magic was fading. The sun, already furnace-hot, was stripping the earth of all color and chiaroscuro. It scraped the living canvas bare, leaving a dry, flat monochrome behind. The world lost all depth and perspective. The white fires faded from the snows on Kilimanjaro. The herds of wild animals began to thin out and disperse.

Where, I wondered, was Patricia now, and what was she doing?

I went inside my bungalow. It consisted of a living-room and a bedroom, furnished in a rudimentary fashion, but perfectly adequate for an outdoor life. From this main building a hedged path, open to the sky, led toward a smaller hut, which contained a kitchen and a bathroom.

Hot water came from an iron boiler, which stood outside on piles of flat stones. Underneath the boiler itself a roaring fire was kept burning by a black servant—doubtless the same "boy" who had informed Patricia that I had refused his services the previous night.

Still thinking about Patricia, I told myself severely. I must stop this obsession at once, and concentrate on my own affairs. Among my papers I had two introductory letters. The first—the official one—I had obtained from Government House in Nairobi: it was addressed to John Bullit, Warden of the Reserve. The other letter, a private one, was for the attention of Bullit's wife: I had obtained it from a school friend of hers whom I had happened to meet just before leaving France.

Outside the bungalow I saw Bogo, my driver, waiting for instructions. The gray cotton uniform with its big flat metal buttons (it belonged to the agency for which he worked) hung in loose folds on his thin, scraggy body. There was an ageless quality about that dull-textured black face; his whole head, with its shaven crown and lined, wrinkled skin, might have belonged to a giant tortoise.

As I gave Bogo my letters of introduction to deliver, I remembered that this taciturn, unforthcoming man, whose whole attitude toward Europeans was one of fierce reserve, had given his friendship and trust to Patricia. I was about to ask him why, but refrained just in time. During two months of close proximity to Bogo, much of it alone up-country, I had not once succeeded in establishing any other than a strictly professional relationship with him. He was, incidentally, most competent at his job.

When he had gone, I looked toward the clearing once more. It was deserted. I felt a strange sense of release, and suddenly realized how hungry and thirsty I was.

Bogo had put our case of provisions in the kitchen. But there was no point in lighting the charcoal stove, or taking down the kitchen implements hanging from the wall. All I needed for my brief stay was one thermos of tea, another of coffee, a few bottles of beer, a flask of whisky, and some biscuits and jam.

I had breakfast on the veranda. The monkey and the gazelle came and kept me company. Nicholas took a dried fig, while Cymbeline accepted a lump of sugar. Kilimanjaro was swathed in heat haze. I had got back my peace of mind.

Bogo returned carrying an envelope. From the lady, he told me.

Sybil Bullit wrote in French, in a tall, sloping, elegant hand. She asked me to come and see her as soon as I possibly could. Right away, if I could manage it.

4

The Warden of the National Park had built his house only a stone's throw from the visitors' compound. But the long, almond-shaped garden in which it stood was entirely surrounded by tall thorn hedges. The bungalow was roofed with brown thatch, and its walls were so dazzling white that they looked freshly whitewashed; while the shutters were painted a quiet pastel green. The paint, you would have said, had only dried the previous day.

The shutters along the front of the building were still closed when I came out from the path through the trees. But my approach must have been anxiously awaited from inside: the door opened before I got to it, and a tall, fair-haired young woman appeared on the threshold. She was wearing dark glasses. Without even giving me time to say hello, she began to speak in English, hurrying and stumbling over her words. She sounded short of breath, probably through trying to say too much at once.

"Sorry to have hurried you like this," she said. "Do please come in—I'm delighted you could get over so quickly—come in, do. It was good of you not to keep me waiting—come inside quick, it's terribly hot out there—"

Sybil Bullit raised one hand to her dark glasses as she spoke, and only lowered it again to push the door shut behind us with a quick, impatient movement.

After the bright sunlight of the bush I found it very dark inside. As we walked down the passage I could hardly see Mrs. Bullit's face, much less that of the native servant who came running out at her approach. She spoke to him in Swahili, with some irritability. He retired, leaving us alone.

"Come on, do," she said to me. "It's so gloomy here."

We went into a big, spacious living-room, which got its light not from the shuttered side of the house, but from windows opening on an inner courtyard. This courtyard was partially roofed in, and the brilliance of the sunlight was still further softened by heavy blue cotton curtains.

Mrs. Bullit's face and body at once relaxed, as if she had found a safe refuge. But she still continued to wear her dark glasses.

"I must apologize for my lack of ceremony," she said. Her voice was now pleasant and intelligent, with a certain impulsive quality about it. "I really am sorry. But if you only knew what Lise means to me—"

She paused for a moment, and then repeated the name, obviously to herself rather than to me, and for the sheer pleasure of speaking it aloud. "Lise," she said. "Lise Darbois."

Then she asked, with sudden nervousness, whether her French pronunciation was still passable.

"From your accent you might be a native," I told her; which was, indeed, quite true. "But I'm less surprised after having read your letter."

A faint blush spread over her cheeks behind the make-up. Since her eyes were still concealed behind those enormous smoked lenses, it was impossible to tell whether this indicated pleasure or embarrassment.

"I hoped that might bring you round a little quicker," she said. Then she took a step toward me and went on: "My God, when I think that scarcely two months ago you were with Lise! Oh, we write to one another quite often, I suppose. I do, certainly. But to find someone who's actually seen and spoken with her—that's quite a different thing—"

She made as though to take my hands in hers, didn't quite manage it, and burst out: "Tell me everything about her, will you? Now, quickly. How is she? What is she doing?"

I tried my hardest to recall every detail of my last encounter with Sybil Bullit's friend—whom, indeed, I only knew very slightly. Rack my memory as I might, though, all I could produce was a vaguely pretty woman, with a certain touch of gaiety about her, but very much the same as many other women of her type and class. A little too nervous and over-sure of herself, I remembered. What rare qualities and peculiar virtues could she possess, in order to arouse such excitement and devotion?

"Well?" Sybil Bullit demanded hungrily. "Go on."

"Well," I said, "Lise is still the French representative of an American cosmetics firm. Since her divorce she's been living a very free sort of life with a painter. I know him rather better than I do her."

"She's happy, of course?"

"I don't really know. I get the impression that she's a bit bored, that she feels she's thrashing around in a void. Sometimes, I think, she envies you your life out here."

Sybil slowly shook her head. Behind the dark glasses her face remained blind and expressionless. Finally she said: "Lise was one of my bridesmaids. We came out to Kenya together. I was married in the white chapel between Nairobi and Naivasha. You probably know it."

"Everybody knows that chapel," I said. It was a tiny sanctuary, of pleasant and unpretentious design, which had been built by Italian P.O.W.'s in their leisure moments while they were working on the construction of the trunk road. The spot they had cleared as a site for the chapel looked out over the vast and magnificent Rift Valley. Six thousand feet below, the river itself spread and crawled, apparently motionless from this great height. It had its source in the heart of Equatorial Africa, and flowed on, mile after mile, till it reached the shores of the Sinai Peninsula.

"You were very lucky," I said. "There can't be a lovelier place in the whole world."

She made no reply; instead she smiled, with all the tender nostalgia that a cherished memory can inspire. And as though she had felt the need of giving full, unrestricted expression to this smile, she took off her dark glasses, slowly and bemusedly, like a sleepwalker.

Why, I asked myself at once, did she keep her eyes hidden? They were dark gray, flecked with golden lights, and very large; the acanthic fold slanted in a tapering point toward her temple on either side. They were her one truly beautiful feature—certainly when, as now, some violent emotion put a sparkling brilliance into them. And *because* of their fresh, shining innocence I suddenly perceived, by sheer contrast, how prematurely youth had fled from her still youthful face. Not even the African sun could tan that sallow, faded complexion. Her hair hung lifeless, and two deep, cracked lines ran down from her forehead, furrowed a path through each cheek, and formed a vertical bracket at both corners of her mouth.

I had an eerie feeling that this face was shared by two completely different women, one of whom owned the eyes, and the other the remaining features. Lise Darbois was not yet thirty. Was it possible that the worn, anaemic countenance confronting me belonged to one of her contemporaries?

Sybil answered my unspoken question without knowing it.

"Lise and I are almost exactly the same age," she told me. "There's only a few weeks' difference between us. We spent five years together in a private school near Lausanne. We were both caught there when war broke out. Lise's parents lived in Paris, and my father was serving in the East Indies. Both of them preferred to leave us where we were during the Occupation."

Sybil gave a tender, curiously youthful laugh, and went on: "I'm sure Lise has told you all about that side of it. What she could never let you know is how ravishingly lovely she was in those days—even as a schoolgirl she dressed and did her hair better than all the rest of us. At fifteen she was a sophisticated Parisian young lady."

Detail after detail, memory piled on memory, Sybil Bullit told me the entire story of her life at this period. I saw now that she had summoned me with such impatience, not so much to make me talk as to have an audience herself.

I gathered that toward the end of the war, Sybil's father had been given an important post in Kenya, and Sybil herself, when going out to join him, had begged Lise Darbois to come with her. She had met Bullit almost on arrival, and this meeting had led them, one fine morning, to the tiny white chapel perched high above the vast magnificence of the Rift Valley.

"Lise went back home almost at once," Sybil concluded, "and soon afterward my father was recalled to London by the Colonial Office, and died there without my ever seeing him again."

She fell silent: I ought to have taken my leave at this point. Sybil had got—indeed, *extracted* might be a more exact description of the process—all she wanted from me, and it was time for me to begin my tour round the Reserve. Yet I still lingered, without being quite sure what kept me there.

"Your husband isn't at home, I take it?" I asked.

◇◇

"He always goes out long before I'm awake, and never comes home at any fixed time," Sybil said, with a vague gesture of one hand. "Only when his animals leave him free."

Once more a silence fell between us; and its full significance was complemented and enhanced by the room in which we sat. The color scheme, indeed, every object visible added something to the over-all feeling of pleasant, civilized security: the honey-colored walls, the indirect light, the bright rush matting on the floor, the engravings in their old-fashioned frames, and the copper flower vases loaded with huge, tropical blooms. Everywhere good taste and the most scrupulous care were apparent. I complimented Sybil on her labors.

She said, in a low voice: "I try to make myself forget that there isn't a single town for over two hundred miles, and that wild beasts of the most dangerous kind can walk up to my front door as and when they please."

Her eyes flickered round her possessions as though they were personal friends. Some of her pieces were certainly very beautiful.

"My husband's parents brought most of this stuff to Africa with them when they settled out here at the turn of the century," Sybil said. "The furniture was a family heirloom."

She paused, as though accidentally, and then added, with careful casualness: "A very ancient family, actually. The senior branch has held a baronetcy since Tudor times."

For an instant her face bore an expression utterly at odds with both her cast of feature and her present life: a smug, bourgeois self-satisfaction. Did this represent some genuine deep-seated feeling, or was it merely another means of inner self-defense, like the furniture and elegant hangings?

She ran her fingers in a mechanical gesture over a tiny rosewood chair, a kind of exquisite toy fashioned in the eighteenth century by some craftsman of real genius.

She said: "My husband sat in that chair when he was a little boy, and his father and grandfather before him. My daughter uses it on occasion, too."

"Patricia!" I exclaimed. Now I knew why I had stayed.

"So you know her name," Sybil said. "Ah, of course: Lise would have told you about her."

This, of course, was not true. I toyed for a moment with the idea of telling her how I had actually met Patricia. But some obscure instinct prompted me to avail myself of the easy white lie that Sybil herself had offered me.

"Do you know what my dream for Patricia is?" Sybil went on brightly. "I'd like to have her educated in France. I want her to learn to dress and behave and carry herself as though she'd been born in Paris. Just as Lise knew how to do."

Sybil's eyes were once more bright with childish excitement and confidence. Then, suddenly, she broke off, shivered, and with a movement so rapid and instinctive that it must have been performed unconsciously, put on her dark glasses again.

Not the slightest sound had heralded the native's approach: I first realized that he was there when he appeared in the middle of the living-room. He was an ancient, wrinkled creature with only one eye, dressed in brown cotton drawers and a torn shirt. It was impossible to tell how tall he was, since he was bent almost double, squatting on deformed shanks. He uttered a few words in Swahili and went out again.

"Kihoro is a Wakamba," Sybil said, in a low, tired voice. "He has been my husband's guide and tracker now for a very long time. He can no longer work as a guard in the Reserve. You saw how badly he's been mauled. So he looks after Patricia. He's been responsible for her since the day she was born, and she's very devoted to him. He's just told me he's taken her her breakfast."

"She's here? Now?" I exclaimed.

"She's just waked up," Sybil said.

"What? But how on earth—"

I stopped short just in time for Sybil to interpret my surprise in her own fashion.

"I know it's rather late," she explained. "But Patricia runs about all day long. She needs plenty of sleep." She looked at me for a moment through her dark glasses, then added: "I'll go and see where she is. You'll be able to talk to her about Lise."

I went to one of the windows on the side where the shutters weren't closed, and drew the curtains back. The window opened on a large patio, round which the living-quarters were spaced. A rudimentary straw-covered colonnade ran round the walls. Sybil walked a little way along it, without a glance at the poinciana, jacarandas, and laburnum that blazed in masses of scarlet, azure, and flame from every corner of the inner court. But instead of making her way immediately to Patricia's room—and despite her morbid dislike for sunlight—Sybil now walked out into the courtyard's open center, where there was no protection against the sheer aching intensity of heat and light. There she paused by a square, formed out of four narrow flower beds, the soil for which had clearly been imported from some distance away. In these beds, watered by tiny irrigation channels, bloomed a few wretched, wilting, colorless flowers—zinnias, petunias, pinks.

Sybil leaned down over these European flowers, straightening a stalk here, trimming a bud there. It was not a genuine solicitude for the plants that inspired her actions: there was a kind of desperate appeal, a prayer almost, latent in them. Was this, too, an apotropaion against solitude, and nothing more?

I was disturbed in my reflections by the sound of a car being driven very fast. It pulled up with a violent squeal of brakes outside the house, on the side where the shuttered wall stared blindly at the sun.

5

The screech of tires on the rough ground was still echoing in the air when the car's driver came into the living-room. Quite obviously he did not expect to find me there. But as soon as he saw me, he instantaneously switched off the amazing and vital energy with which he had swept into the room—an achievement which his very considerable height and bulk in no way impeded. He did it with the sort of easy skill displayed by professional exponents of muscular balance, such as dancers, boxers, or acrobats.

He was carrying a *kiboko,* a long rhinoceros-hide whip, in one hand.

"How do you do?" he said. Despite its harsh tone his voice had a clear, bluff, honest quality about it. "Glad to see you. My name's John Bullit: I'm the Warden of this Reserve."

I was about to introduce myself, but he went on: "I know, I know. Your name's in the book. And as you're our only guest at the moment—"

He left the sentence unfinished, and instead asked me if I would like a whisky. Without waiting for my reply, he tossed his *kiboko* into a chair and marched off in the direction of the cocktail cabinet, on the far side of the room.

For so full-bodied and powerful a man, he was quite extraordinarily handsome. He was very tall and long in the leg; the flesh that covered his big bones, though thick-textured and perhaps even on the heavy side, was no hindrance to the speed and suppleness of his movements. This firm, dynamic substance was, quite simply, the source of his vitality, the storehouse from which his energies were refueled. The sun which had burned his skin till he looked the color of fumed oak could not penetrate beneath it.

His clothes revealed more of his smooth, muscular body than they actually covered. He wore an old pair of shorts, cut high above the knee, and the sleeves of his ancient bush shirt were rolled up well beyond his elbows. This garment hung open from throat to waistband, leaving the whole of his chest exposed.

◇◇

"Cheers," Bullit said. Before drinking he held the glass under his slightly snub nose and sniffed the bouquet of the whisky. His fine nostrils dilated and contracted rapidly. He thrust out his square mustache a little: a long, pink, mobile underlip protruded beneath it. Thick, tangled hair, somewhere between auburn and pure red in color, curled over his heavy forehead and grew in sideburns down full, hard cheeks. It was more of an animal's muzzle, a mask, than a human face. But his solid, sculptured features and striking appearance combined to give him an extraordinary power to charm those with whom he came in contact.

"I'm sorry I haven't had time to attend to you this morning," Bullit told me, between two gulps of whisky. "Fact is, it was still dark when I left the house. Urgent business. Had a report about some shady native characters turning up in a deserted corner of the Reserve. Often get poachers round that area. You can still raise a pretty good price on ivory—the tusks, y'know. And ground-up rhino horn is highly valued in the Far East as an aphrodisiac. These bloody Hindu boxwallahs we've got swarming about the place act as middlemen. There are always some bastards who try and shoot my elephants and rhinos with their poisoned arrows—Wakamba, Kipsigui, any other tribe—"

"Did you catch them this time?" I asked.

"No. False alarm." Bullit stared regretfully at the terrible whip he had thrown down as he came in. "Oh, there *were* natives there, all right, but they were Masai."

Bullit's hoarse voice betrayed that remarkable note of respect that I had observed among all the English in Kenya when they mentioned this redoubtable warrior tribe.

"The Masai," he went on, "aren't tradesmen. They neither sell nor buy anything. It's a pity they're blacks;
they've got the instincts of gentlemen."

He gave a short bark of laughter, and added: "Still,
gentlemen or not, I can't have them going after my lions."

There are certain men with whom it is useless wasting
time over the normal polite preliminaries that etiquette
demands at a first meeting. Since such men create their
own world, outside all social conventions, politenesses
have no meaning for them, and they draw you at once into
their own ambience. So I said to Bullit: "*Your* lions, *your*
rhinos, *your* elephants. These wild beasts seem to be your
personal possessions as far as you're concerned."

"They belong to the Crown," Bullit replied. "And I am
the Crown's representative here."

"I don't really think," I said, "that your attitude is entirely a product of your sense of duty."

Bullit abruptly put down his glass, which was still half
full, and began to stride up and down the room. Yet his
big, bulky body never so much as brushed against a piece
of furniture, and his heavy mosquito boots made no sound
on the floor. When he had taken several turns to and fro
he said, still going on with his silent, cat-like pacing:
"After I'd dealt with the Masai, I spent a couple of hours
in the bush, putting down salt at the animals' favorite
feeding-grounds. They're fond of salt. It adds to their
strength. Doubtless you will tell me that I was prompted
to do this by something over and above my sense of duty."

To and fro he went across the cluttered-up room: his
long, regular, springy, silent stride was now perceptibly
faster.

"And what about the dams I dig, and the irrigation

channels I construct to make sure that every district has its reservoir throughout the year? That's not an obligatory duty, either. Nor do I have any compunction about turning tourists out of the Reserve—supposing, for example, that they drive through blasting away on their horns, and shake the animals' confidence that this is *their* domain."

Bullit suddenly stopped dead in mid-stride, close to me, with that muscular self-control I had already remarked in him.

"All the rights and privileges here belong to the animals," he barked. "I want to see them left in peace. Secure from want. Protected from man. Happy. And I'll do my damndest to see that that's the way it is, do you hear?"

I glanced uneasily at his dilated, unwinking eyes. What had provoked this abrupt and violent outburst? It seemed very unlikely that I was his real target; my innocent remark had merely served as a convenient excuse for bringing to a head some long-festering crisis. At what or whom, I wondered, was his tormented fury *really* directed? Whom was he striking at through me?

The violent emotion suddenly faded from Bullit's face. He raised his head, ears cocked—a gesture which brought his clipped, square mustache to somewhere about the middle of my forehead. Then he picked up his glass again and drained it at a single gulp. It was then that I caught the light footsteps which he had heard several seconds earlier. When Sybil came into the room, her husband's face was calm and relaxed.

6

They came together so spontaneously that their behavior seemed unconnected with any conscious act of will. When they met in the middle of the room Bullit put one of his huge, powerful hands on Sybil's shoulder, covering it completely, and drew her to him. With the other hand—and there was an unexpected gentleness about the gesture—he took off her dark glasses. Then his great auburn head, so like a wild beast's muzzle, bent toward her pale face, and he kissed her eyelids. Instantly the tension went out of Sybil's body. She swayed, pressing herself forward close against his huge muscular torso as though she wanted to melt into it. This demonstration of affection took place so quickly, and was so fundamentally wholesome, that I felt neither shame nor embarrassment at being a witness to it. The behavior of Bullit and his wife was so sincere and natural that it entirely avoided any possible charge of tactlessness.

A wife and husband who had been separated all day by their several duties were now reunited, and had kissed each other. That was all. What was there to hide? But this I knew: watching the gestures and expressions of Sybil and her husband, I saw in them, beyond any shadow of doubt, a shining proof of all that love can bring to two people, once and forever. I saw there tenderness, integrity, certainty: everything that a man and a woman can desire and get, each from the other, to soothe away their deepest sorrows or perplexities, and to share in a true, heaven-made marriage.

I found myself thinking about the little white chapel standing in the bush at the edge of the Rift Valley's wild splendors. It was here that Bullit had married Sybil. It was not hard to picture the naïve solemnity, the absolute faith and trust, the enchanted solitude à *deux* which they carried with them on that day. Since then ten years had passed. But nothing had changed for them, or between them: and so it would continue till the end of their life together, while a single breath of life still animated her pale, exhausted face and his big, ruddy, half-animal countenance under its thatch of auburn hair.

This embrace, with its simple, complete gesture of release and protectiveness, only lasted a few brief seconds. Bullit and Sybil drew apart almost as soon as they had kissed. But it was not till Sybil's eye actually caught mine afterward that she remembered my presence. Then the glow of happiness abruptly faded in her lovely eyes, and she drew on her dark glasses with that automatic gesture I had already come to know well. The lines down her cheek seemed deeper: she shivered. Once again her nerves were strained nearly to the breaking-point. Yet, so far as I could see, nothing which Sybil had told me could justify such a dramatic transformation.

"I'm terribly sorry," she said. "I couldn't persuade Patricia to come in here. You must forgive her. She isn't used to normal social behavior."

Bullit had not shifted. His big features were still settled in a calm, tranquil expression. But I saw, watching him, that he had become peculiarly alert and attentive

He seemed to me well aware of the impalpable tension that had made itself felt in the atmosphere: that indefinable something which enables a stranger, on occasion, to surmise the return to a conscious level of some old, persistent, secret bone of contention between two long-married and mutually devoted people.

I laughed, and said: "After all, the child's been brought up in the wilds of Kilimanjaro. It's quite natural for her not to want any contact with people like me. She has nothing to do with the world we come from."

Bullit's face broke into a grateful smile. This reaction was no less emphatic than his burst of anger had been a few minutes before, and seemed to me equally exaggerated and devoid of any reasonable basis.

"That's right," he said mildly. "It's quite natural."

Sybil cried out, her lower lip trembling a little as she spoke: "But John—if we let things go on like this, what will happen? If Patricia continues to live here, she'll turn into an impossible little savage. We've got to do *something.*"

Bullit's voice became gentler still. "We tried once, darling. Remember? School simply made the child ill."

"She was two years younger then," Sybil persisted. "It's a different proposition today. We must think about the child's future."

Two feverish patches of color flushed up red on either cheek.

Then, abruptly, she dragged me into the argument.

"Don't you agree," she said, "that one day Patricia will be the first person to blame us for her poor education?"

Bullit made no comment; but his oddly pale eyes, with

their network of fine red veins (sunshine or over-drink-
ing?), never left mine. With every ounce of strength he
possessed, his look proclaimed to me, he was willing me to
give the opposite answer to that for which his wife hoped.
Each of them, according to their natures was trying to
enroll me as a supporter in this vital argument. And to
what end? To settle the future position of a small girl in
gray overalls, a small girl who belonged to a dawn world
inhabited by beasts of prey.

How could a casual guest possibly take sides in such
a case? I thought of Patricia, with her urchin's haircut. It was this private memory, and this alone, which
finally made up my mind. Patricia's parents could not
possibly know what had influenced my decision. In a
cheerfully casual voice, which suggested that the real
point of the discussion had gone over my head, I remarked: "I'm always on the child's side; it's probably because I've never had any of my own. I'm afraid my sym-
pathies are all with Patricia."

There was a brief silence. Then Sybil produced a very
artificial smile, and said: "Please forgive us for dragging
you into our family problems. You didn't come all this
way just for that."

"Too true," Bullit observed. He was smiling himself, but
as a man might after meeting an old and trusted friend
whom he hadn't seen for years. "I'll show you round
the Reserve myself," he went on, half-raising one enormous paw as though to slap me on the back. "I can show
you some sights that very few people have ever seen."

Then he glanced at his wife, who seemed at this moment very far away from us, and added, almost timidly:

"Why don't you come too, darling? Just this once, in honor of our guest. It will be like old times—and I'm sure it'd do you good."

Sybil made no reply to this; instead, she suddenly said to me: "My God! What *will* Lise think when she hears you haven't met Patricia?"

"Lise?" Bullit asked, puzzled. "Why *Lise?*"

"Our guest is a friend of hers," Sybil explained. "I never had a moment to tell you. Lise gave him a letter of introduction to me, and of course he and Lise will be seeing one another again very soon."

Every time Sybil uttered Lise's name her voice seemed more lively and her face younger. Bullit's features, on the other hand, seemed to become somehow remote: he withdrew himself behind an invisible barrier. There was no trace left in either of them of that friendliness which he had shown me a moment ago.

"When are you leaving?" Sybil asked me.

"Tomorrow," Bullit said, forestalling my reply with almost open rudeness. "That's what's down in the book, anyway."

"Tomorrow?" Sybil exclaimed. "So soon? Then I must begin my letter to Lise right away. There are so many things I want to tell her. You know, since I've met you I feel she's much more real—much nearer me—"

Bullit went and poured himself another whisky.

"I haven't even offered you any proper entertainment," Sybil ran on. "You must come back this evening and have a nice cosy tea party with us. There won't be anything else for you to do, in any case—John's forbidden vehicles to move about the Reserve after dark, haven't you, John?"

Bullit muttered something about the headlights dazzling the animals.

"I'd be delighted to come," I told Sybil. "There's no immediate hurry about your letter. My driver can collect it tomorrow, before we leave."

Bullit stared at me for a moment over his full glass of Scotch.

"Will you kindly tell me," he inquired with some abruptness, "why this driver of yours spent the night in his car when there was a bed at his disposal in the servants' quarters? I suppose this fine Nairobi gentleman is too high and mighty to sleep under the same roof as a bunch of up-country niggers."

"It wasn't like that at all," I said. "Bogo and I have made a very long circular trip together, as far as Lake Kivu. All the hotels refused accommodation to natives, except in filthy little kennels. Bogo got into the habit of sleeping in the car. He may be a simple, primitive creature, but he has a sense of dignity."

"Dignity," Bullit repeated through his teeth. *"Dignity!"* His eyes wandered toward the long rhinoceros-hide whip hanging over the arm of a chair; then returned to contemplate the bottom of his whisky glass.

"I was born in Rhodesia," he said suddenly. "My father was a District Officer, in charge of a very large area. When I was fourteen I went on my first safari, with another boy of the same age. One day we found ourselves in lion country, where hunting was strictly forbidden. Suddenly, we saw a bush move. The official ban notwithstanding, we fired, and one of us scored a hit. But our victim turned out to be a native, dead as a doornail. We went off and reported the accident to the Chief of the

nearest village. An old Negro—" here Bullit raised his
eyes and glanced quickly at me—"of considerable dignity. He said: 'You're very lucky it wasn't a lion. Your
father would never have forgiven you.' And that was true
enough; my father had the law in his blood."

"John, why do you rake up these old stories?" Sybil
said, in a low voice. "You know how I hate them. And
honestly, they make you sound like a savage yourself."

Bullit drank up without answering, went and picked
up his *kiboko*, and said to me: "If you don't mind, I've
got some work to do now. I'll detail a guard to show you
round the Reserve." He did not look at me as he spoke.
Then he stretched himself, arms folded, and the room
suddenly seemed much smaller.

"John," Sybil said quickly, "promise me you'll do one
thing. Tell Patricia to stop behaving so badly, and make
her come and have tea with us. Whatever happens, our
guest must be able to discuss her with Lise when he gets
home."

The vast fist clutching the rawhide whip tightened its
grip on the stock. Then it relaxed once more. Bullit's
shaggy great head, like that of a sick, unhappy animal,
bent down toward his wife. Then he said, very tenderly:
"I promise, darling." His lips brushed her hair. She pressed
herself against him and he held her as close, and as lov-
ingly, as he had done earlier.

❀

7

I left Sybil a few moments later, and she made no effort to stop me going. Her entire mind was concentrated on the letter she was about to write, and the effect it would have on its recipient.

As I came out of the bungalow, the fierce, blinding heat dazzled and half-stunned me with the violence of its impact. I stopped despite myself. Bullit was standing, bareheaded, beside his vehicle (a mud-spattered Land Rover) and giving instructions to Kihoro, his tracker. This was the scarred, lame, one-eyed old native I had seen earlier. Bullit pretended not to notice me; but Kihoro shot me a quick, piercing glance with his one eye, and began to gabble something at great speed to his master. I turned away and walked off in the direction of my bungalow.

I had reached the edge of the clearing, and was just about to plunge into the thorny maqui which bordered it, when a long, obviously human shadow appeared beside mine. I stopped, and found Bullit standing at my elbow.

I experienced a curious, instantaneous feeling of *coolness*: Bullit's body was so broad and big that it protected me from the sun. But at the same time I felt an uneasy qualm at the way in which he had padded silently after me and—as always—taken me off my guard. Why had he done it this time? What did he still hope to get out of me?

Presumably with the intention of avoiding my gaze, he

was staring up at the tall, thorny trees that towered behind my head. His arms hung motionless at his sides, but the tips of his fingers drummed nervously on his bare, bronzed thighs. I noticed that his nails were cut short and kept scrupulously clean. He seemed uneasy. Finally he said, coughing: "If you like, we can stroll along together. I'm going to the native village, and your compound is on the way."

He walked like a native beater, with quick easy steps, bending forward a little as he moved. I could hardly keep up with him: very quickly we found ourselves in the heart of the bush. Then Bullit suddenly stopped and spun round on his heel to face me, completely blocking the narrow path. His arms were very slightly bent, and his clenched fists held in at hip level. His red-veined eyes stared fixedly into mine, and there were deep lines visible on his forehead, between the thatch of auburn hair and the heavy, reddish eyebrows. I thought, stupidly enough in all conscience, that he was about to attack me and knock me out. This may have been a lunatic notion; but then I was beginning to find something decidedly lunatic about Bullit's general behavior.

A heavy silence, to which the earth, the heat, and the tall trees surrounding us all contributed, hung in the air between us. Somehow it had to be broken.

"What's the matter?" I asked.

Bullit said, slowly and softly: "You were out near the big water hole this morning."

The man standing in front of me was, physically speaking, a very dangerous proposition; and I could not understand, much less foresee, any of his moods or impulses. Nevertheless, my first instinctive thought was that Patricia had betrayed me. This hurt me so acutely that I said, despite myself: "You mean to say that your daughter informed on me—"

"Her?" said Bullit, shrugging, "I haven't seen her since yesterday."

"But nevertheless you still know that I was where I had no business to be, don't you? And that she was with me?"

"That was exactly what I want to talk to you about," Bullit said. He hesitated, the perplexed lines on his forehead deepening under the wiry russet hair. Then he said, in some irritation: "I don't know how on earth to put this business to you."

"Listen, I can honestly swear I had no idea that the area was out of bounds to visitors. But if you feel it's your duty to turn me out, well, I'm quite ready to leave in an hour's time instead of staying till tomorrow. Fair enough?"

Bullit shook his head and smiled, in a nervous, unpremeditated way, which gave a strange charm to his wild beast's features.

"Even supposing I wanted to throw you out," he said, "how could I possibly do it? Sybil's already all worked up by the idea of her special tea party. She doesn't often have an opportunity for that sort of thing, poor dear."

Then, his embarrassment suddenly gone, Bullit said, with a fine frankness and simplicity that exactly matched his outward physical appearance: "Thank you. I'm truly grateful to you for not telling my wife you saw Patricia early this morning—and, more especially, for not saying *where* you saw her."

Bullit wiped his perspiring face with the back of his

hand. I had previously seen him come back from a long walk in the blazing sun without a single drop of sweat on him; and in any case we were standing in the shade of the huge thorn trees. I hardly knew what kind of response to make to this unexpected tribute.

A few yards away from us an impala suddenly bounded across the path. A few birds flew up out of the undergrowth, and in the treetops, I could hear the monkeys chattering.

Bullit said: "If my wife had any idea what Pat gets up to every morning, I don't know what—"

He broke off, fumbling for words, wiped his forehead again, and concluded, lamely: "It'd make things very difficult for everyone concerned."

He stood there a moment longer, shifting from one foot to the other, scratching his head under its thick mat of auburn hair.

"What I'm trying to find out," Bullit said, not looking at me, "is why you *didn't* say anything. You weren't in the picture. Did Sybil tell you something privately that put you on your guard?"

"Certainly not. And I'm by no means certain myself just why I kept quiet. I think the truth of it is that I felt my meeting with your daughter was a secret between the two of us."

"But why should it have been?"

"Why?" I echoed, and caught myself up short, afraid of being laughed at. And then, with the scent and the small crackling noises of the bush all around me, perhaps too because I sensed a certain animal simplicity about Bullit himself, I took the plunge and told him everything. I described the instinctive urge that had driven me to seek out the wild beasts in their fantastic meeting-place at the foot of Kilimanjaro. I admitted my desperate longing for their friendship, and the impossibility of ever attaining it as far as I was concerned; and I told how a little girl in gray overalls had, for a few brief moments, won me access to their kingdom.

At first, still embarrassed to be making this kind of confession, I kept my eyes fixed on the dry, thorny undergrowth at my feet; and all I could see of Bullit were his legs, great sturdy columns the color of baked clay. Nevertheless, his heavy, concentrated breathing hinted at the intensity of his interest in my story, and this gradually removed my embarrassment. After a while I raised my head, and addressed him directly. Not a muscle stirred in his face as he listened, but his expression was one of incredulous delight. When I had finished he said, slowly and awkwardly: "Then—I mean—*you* feel there's something between Pat and the animals—*you*, a town-dweller—something special, something that mustn't, can't be disturbed—don't you?"

He fell silent, one hand unconsciously going up to scrabble in his hair again. At the same time, it struck me, he was examining my appearance in a completely new way, as though hunting for some hidden blemish or mark of deformity.

"But, in that case," he burst out finally, "how in heaven's name can you be a friend of Lise Darbois?"

"I'm not," I said. "Far from it. I scarcely know her; and from the little I've seen, even that degree of acquaintance strikes me as undesirable."

The nervous, indecisive, and distinctly charming smile I had already observed now broke out again on Bullit's face.

"Come on," I said, "own up. You'd have been delighted to lay into me with that rhino whip of yours, simply and solely on account of that young lady, wouldn't you?"

"Too bloody true I would," Bullit said, with classic simplicity. Then he suddenly exploded into a tremendous, ingenuous burst of laughter that seemed to fill the whole forest. At this moment he seemed half child, half ogre. Between two convulsive snorts of mirth, he gasped again: "Too bloody true. I'd have taken the *kiboko* to you all right!" Nearly out of breath, he repeated the word *kiboko* several times, till his hysteria became contagious, and I too thought this word one of the funniest things I had ever heard. Then I began to laugh with him, and we stood there on the bush track, facing each other still, laughing till the tears ran down our cheeks. It was at this moment that the first spark of real friendship was kindled between us.

When the paroxysms died down, and Bullit began talking to me again, his tone was completely different. Now he treated me as an intimate, who knew all the hidden secrets of his home life.

"Who would suppose," he said, with controlled violence, "that a stupid, empty-headed doll like Lise could do us so much harm from eight thousand odd miles away?"

"Without meaning to, or even having any notion of her effect on you," I put in.

Bullit shook his head obstinately. "That makes no difference," he said. "I still hate her guts. The only thing

I'm interested in is the happiness of Sybil and our child."

He swung round and set off down the track once more; but his movements were slower now, and his head was bent in thought. After thrashing out his ideas for a while he began to talk again, without turning round. His broad back completely blotted out the view for me, and his words marched in time with our footsteps.

"Don't think I'm completely mad because I let Pat run wild in the bush and mingle with the animals as she pleases," he said. "To begin with, she undoubtedly *does* have an uncanny power over them. That's something that's either there or not: nothing to be done about it. You can know animals like the back of your hand and still not have that basic *rapport* with them. Take me, for example. I've lived among wild beasts all my life, but it's hopeless to pretend I've got the touch. It's something you're born with, and Pat has it."

I hurried after Bullit's huge retreating figure, trying to tread exactly in his footsteps so as not to disturb this revelatory vein. The slow, hoarse voice talked on, taking me further into Patricia's mysterious world.

"I've known several men who had the gift," Bullit said. "One or two were Europeans. Most were natives. But none of them could hold a candle to Pat. She was born with it. Besides, she's been brought up among wild animals. Most important of all—" Bullit hesitated very slightly at this point—"she's never harmed them in any way. They *understand* each other. There's an alliance between them."

There was one question I could not resist asking at this point. "Is that a sufficient guarantee of her safety?"

"She thinks so," Bullit said, still striding ahead with

his back to me. "And she ought to know better than we do. But I haven't got her innocent faith; so I have her watched by Kihoro."

"That crippled old tracker?" I exclaimed.

"Don't get any mistaken ideas about *him*," Bullit said, quickening his pace. "Kihoro may be a cripple, but he can move faster than a leopard when he needs to. And more quietly. If I went round spying on her Patricia would hear me at once—even though I know the game well. But Kihoro is always just behind her shadow, and she never suspects a thing. It doesn't matter about his having only one eye, either; he's quicker and more accurate with a gun than I am—and I'm reckoned to be one of the best shots in East Africa."

Bullit turned round. There was an unfamiliar light in his eye, and his voice sounded suddenly younger.

"Do you know, there was a time once when Kihoro never asked for more than one cartridge, no matter what dangerous beast he was stalking—lion, elephant, even buffalo? And—"

Bullit broke off abruptly, gnawing with savage violence at his lower lip, as though to punish himself for some fault which had escaped my notice.

"Don't worry," he said. "His cartridge pouches are always full when he goes out to guard Pat."

The path became wider at this point, and we walked side by side in silence for a little.

I said: "It was obviously Kihoro who told you about my meeting with Patricia."

"Yes. But it's vital that she shouldn't know he's always watching her. It would completely spoil her private game. And *that's* the only real pleasure she can get around here."

◇◇

We were approaching a group of huts which certainly wasn't the visitors' compound. Without noticing, I had accompanied Bullit as far as the native village.

8

A score or so of straw shacks, camouflaged by high thorny scrub, served as living-quarters for the staff of the Reserve —guards, bearers, kitchen workers—together with their families. More solidly constructed buildings housed an electric generator, a workshop for general repairs, a gasoline dump, and a store for clothing and food supplies.

The occupants of this little village swarmed out and surrounded Bullit the moment he appeared. The rangers were in uniform; khaki drill tunics with big metal buttons, shorts and pork-pie forage caps of the same material, and cartridge belts strapped round their waists. The mechanics wore greasy old rags, while the bearers sported long white tunics, nipped in at the waist with broad blue cummerbunds. The clerks were dressed in European clothes, even down to a collar and tie. The women's cotton wraps presented a cheerful spectrum of bright, crude, primary colors, most of which clashed excruciatingly with each other. The children were stark naked.

There was no doubt about the kind of welcome Bullit got. The giant, red-headed Warden was immensely popular in the village. Shouts of delight, even impromptu songs greeted him. A warm, ingenuous affection shone from all these beaming black faces. Bullit glanced significantly at me. *You see how it is,* his expression seemed to say. *Despite the* kiboko *and my unfortunate adventure in Rhodesia: you see how it is.*

In his eyes I could see crystallized all the absolute self-assurance and moral certainty which I had found, on countless occasions, in the spoken assumptions of old colonial administrators and their sons: the natural superiority of the white races, the natural inferiority of these childish, primitive people, who neither valued nor respected (they said) any argument except physical force. I was unable to share these beliefs. They had only possessed any cogency as long as the indigenous population took them for granted. But that day was long past. One or two individual Europeans might appear to justify these assumptions, by virtue of their powerful personalities and a kind of instinctive superiority. It was, too, in just such isolated, Godforsaken districts as this one that modern social progress had made least progress. The time was coming—had, indeed, come—when the relationship between men of different color would have to be radically revised. But it would have been pure waste of time (and I had little enough time to spare) for me to argue this point with Bullit. He wouldn't listen to a word I said; he had his own notions of the eternal verities well-established already.

Now he fended off the noisy crowd with great good-humor, swiping every head within range, and gently rolling naked, delighted pickaninnies over in the dust with the toe of his boot. Then he got the rangers on parade, and instantly the whole atmosphere changed. The guards stood to attention, silent and motionless, arms stiffly by their sides, heels together, while he gave them their orders. Then they dismissed to their huts.

"I'd better fill you in," Bullit said. "Those chaps have been told not to let any Masai out of their sight for a single moment during the next week. Till they move on, in fact."

"You allow these Masai to camp in the Reserve?"

"Oh, we've got to tolerate them up to a point. The district's belonged to them since God knows when, and they're no trouble really. They stick to their prescribed grazing-grounds."

"Then why do you need to keep such a close eye on them?"

"To protect the lions," Bullit said. "The traditional ambition of every Masai, the achievement that will win him the highest renown, is to kill a lion, with spear and knife alone. The practice is officially forbidden throughout the Colony; but that doesn't stop them having a go on the quiet. Many of them never come back. They don't care—" Bullit shrugged his shoulders—"nor do I. A few blacks the less, even Masai—well. But I have no intention of letting them harm my lions."

The rangers came out of their huts: their cartridge belts were full, and they carried carbines. They went off into the bush, chattering, in great high spirits.

I was about to set off back to my own bungalow when Bullit said: "Don't go for a minute. I've got something to check up over there—generators."

He vanished into a small shed: I heard the thud of diesel engines.

Then—quickly, silently, and doubtless in accordance

with a well-conceived plan that had been executed on several earlier occasions—the pickaninnies swarmed out of hiding, and gathered on both sides of the shed door. When Bullit came out, they fell on him again.

This time Bullit pretended to be taken by surprise, to be hard put to defend himself. Boys and girls clustered over him like bunches of black grapes, hanging on to his boots, his knees, and the bottoms of his shorts, shrieking with delight. The whole village turned out to watch the fun. Huge teeth gleamed, dazzling white, in the black grinning faces.

Suddenly I saw a familiar bowl-shaped haircut bobbing energetically through the crowd. A small, disheveled demon materialized behind Bullit's back, and yelling like a savage, forced the native children to relinquish their grip for a moment. Then she sprang at Bullit's back, grabbed him by the neck, and swung herself up onto one shoulder. It had all happened so quickly—and anyway she was now wearing a new pair of overalls, faded blue this time—that it was only at this point that I recognized Patricia's characteristic features, in particular her slender neck and urchin haircut. As Bullit had his back to me, I could not see the expression on his daughter's face; but it was not hard to guess from her movements. With her left hand she grabbed Bullit's chin, and squeezed it as though she would choke him. With her right she snatched off his big bush hat. Then she plunged both hands into his thick auburn hair, pulling and kneading it.

For Patricia, words were now superfluous: her every gesture proclaimed her fierce affection and triumphant possessiveness. Look at this noble giant, she seemed to say, this Warden of a National Park. Look at him well: he belongs to me, and to no one else. I can do what I like with him.

And Bullit, with Patricia's heels hammering in his ribs, and his head going round both literally and metaphorically, accepted the horse's role thus thrust upon him. He pranced and curveted, arching his neck and laughing delightedly.

Patricia gazed round her audience, face flushed with pride and excitement. Suddenly her expression froze. Had she spotted me? She slid down Bullit's body as though he were a tree, flung herself on the pickaninnies, and dragged them after her. They all rolled on the ground in a confused heap.

Bullit picked up his bush hat; but before putting it on, he ran one big hand very gently through his disordered hair, which Patricia's attentions had reduced to a wild tangle. A vague, abstracted smile, full of pride and adoration, spread over his face.

"Come on," he said to me, after a moment or so. "I'll see you home."

Regretfully I turned away from that whirlwind of red dust and black bodies where a pair of pastel-blue overalls could still be glimpsed, momentarily, through the *mêlée*.

9

My bungalow—though I had not realized this—was in fact quite near at hand. The native village and the visitors' compound were completely hidden from each other by forest and scrub: each formed a private domain, invisible and apparently inaccessible from the other.

As we reached the veranda steps I asked Bullit if he would like a drink. Without waiting for his reply (a trick I had learned from him) I went in and opened a bottle of whisky.

It was nearly midday. The light fell vertically, beyond the open veranda, like a sheet of incandescent metal. The tree shadows had shrunk to nothing, leaving the ground bare, and baking.

We drank in a comfortable, friendly silence. Here, in the center of a blazing universe which seemed about to reach fusion point at any moment, two men sat together under the same roof, sharing a common condition of relaxed and delicious idleness, with the same alcoholic magic warming their palates and coursing through their blood streams. Two men who felt in physical harmony with one another, and saw their friendship growing of its own accord.

"Pity you're off so soon," Bullit said, his voice slurred and barely audible. "Great pity. Y'couldn't stay, I suppose?"

"Impossible. Got a seat booked on the plane." My lips moved just enough to articulate the words.

Bullit sighed. "And just when I had an agreeable guest for once—" He drank what was left of his whisky and sat contemplating his glass. I refilled it.

"Tourists," he said. "You've simply no idea what they can be like."

Slowly, between sips of whisky, he told me about them. There was the lady who insisted on taking all her jewelry when camping at the foot of Kilimanjaro, only to see a monkey run off with it from her breakfast table one morning. There were the guests who complained because their bungalows weren't equipped with refrigerators, and, at the opposite extreme, the adventurous-minded types who took their camp beds out into the bush. There were also the optimistic luxury-hunters, who expected the Reserve to be something like the famous Treetops Hotel in Nyeri. What they wanted was to sit up aloft on specially constructed platforms, drinking champagne, and watching the animals by floodlight. And there were the lovers, who showed a well-marked tendency to play lion-and-tiger fantasies with each other.

"And when you think," Bullit concluded, his voice somewhat more animated now, "that if one of these creatures, either through stupidity, awkwardness, or bloody-minded conceit, breaks any of the rules, and, as a result, is attacked by a wild animal, it's the *animal* that my rangers have to kill—!"

"What would you do," I inquired, "if this wasn't one of your duties?"

Bullit parried this. "The only good thing about knowing your exact duties," he observed, "is that it means you don't have to worry about that kind of problem."

I was about to reply, but he abruptly motioned me to keep quiet. Then he pointed with one finger, out and up, beyond the veranda. Following his indication, I saw, protruding above the branches of an acacia tree (and looking as though it were attached to them), a most remarkable head that moved with delicate grace from leaf to leaf. It was slender and tapering, with flat, ingenuous features, dappled here and there the color of pale leather. Its ears were neat little triangles, set sharply erect; and it had long, thick, voluptuous eyelashes, as black and silky as an odalisque's. It was, in fact, a young giraffe, picking its food with most circumspect elegance from among the thorns and prickles. Behind it I could see a second, even larger, specimen.

"The mother," Bullit whispered.

I saw an immense neck, its texture that of watered silk, swaying slowly to and fro like a tree trunk in a gale. The big giraffe now decided to browse from the same tree as its offspring, and the two of them presented a remarkable picture as they stood there side by side. The mother's head was an exact, though much larger, copy of the one I had first noticed; she had the same dappled muzzle, pricked ears, and enormous eyelashes, which gave the impression of having been painted with mascara. I contemplated this gentle two-headed monster in fascinated amazement.

The two heads, one after the other, slowly worked their way down from branch to branch till they vanished altogether.

"You see how trusting and happy the wild creatures are here," Bullit said. "Giraffes are generally reckoned one of the most shy and easily frightened species. Yet they habitually wander right up to the bungalows."

Bullit's chin was resting on his fist as he spoke: the fist seemed bigger than ever, and the jaw more square and solid. The whisky he had just drunk inflamed the tiny red veins in his eyes. Yet the great brick-red face was radiant with a kind of luminous happiness, the shy hope of seeing a private vow fulfilled. It was almost unbelievable.

"Odd mug for a wild animals' wet nurse, eh?" said my companion, disconcertingly.

"Well," I temporized, "that isn't the side of you they talk about in Nairobi. You're the great Bull Bullit there."

"Bull Bullit, eh?" said the Warden, heavily. His chin settled further into his fist, and his face became expressionless. "That's a nickname I haven't heard in a long while."

"It fits you very well, though," I said.

He slowly raised his big, taurine head. "Oh, I know that," he remarked. "I did my best to make it famous, too. Bull Bullit the ivory-poacher, with a side line in rhino horns. Bull Bullit the professional hunter, the hired gunman, the man who exterminated big game throughout God knows how many Districts—"

"That's certainly the legend that's stuck to you all over East Africa," I said.

Bullit said: "Legend? It was the sober truth." He got to his feet in one quick movement, and gripped the balustrade of the veranda with both hands. It shook and groaned protestingly beneath those huge fingers.

"What else could I do?" he cried. The words were not so much addressed to me as to the clearing, the pool, and Kilimanjaro itself, still and neutral now in this still, neutral light. He came back to the table and sat down.

"I was given a gun," he said, "as a bribe to make me learn my ABC's. My father took me on safari before I was ten. Instead of bedtime stories I had tales of hunting and legendary hunters. I was stuffed and gorged with the big-game legend. They taught me to track animals like a native, and to shoot between the eyes if I couldn't sight behind the shoulder for a shot to the heart. And then, when I decided to become a professional hunter, my father quite suddenly did an about-face. He was furious at the idea. He insisted on packing me off to school in England. No ifs or buts."

Up to this point Bullit had been talking more to himself than to me. But now he addressed me personally.

"Can you imagine what that meant?" he demanded. "No more camp fires, no more sunlit days in the bush, no more wild game roving freely around me. Instead, I would have a narrow life divided between dormitory, dining-hall, class-rooms, and prep. There was only one way out for me, and I took it. I ran away from home, with a rifle and cartridge belt, determined to make a livelihood by using them. And so I did; a good one."

With these final words a heavy note of melancholy crept into Bullit's voice. He sat in silence for a while. On his face was that dreamy, incredulous, nostalgic expression that old men assume when they mull over their youthful joys and follies, as though observing the actions of a totally different person. Yet Bullit himself was not yet forty.

It was not too difficult to guess at the memories that were passing through his uncomplicated mind. His earlier career as adventurer and ivory-hunter was a legend that had spread from the shores of the Indian Ocean to the great African lakes. Anywhere you went, from the Nairobi bars to a Uganda hotel, or the big estates in Tanganyika and Kivu, you could always find men ready to tell you about the fabulous Bull Bullit, as he had been in his heyday. One would speak of his physical strength and powers of endurance; another of his incredible stubbornness; a third of his audacity, a fourth of his marksmanship and uncanny tracking skill. Each would back up his opinion with really staggering anecdotes.

They spoke of herds of elephants that Bullit had decimated, for the sake of the ivory that Indian middlemen shipped abroad to the Far East; and of countless buffalo, slaughtered and sold to the natives for their meat; and of lions and tigers, shot down for the price their skins would fetch. They recounted missions that Bullit had undertaken for the Government, clearing wild beasts from certain areas where they were proving a real menace. There were tales of vigils without number in treetop *machans,* which destroyed man-eaters and cattle-killers, and freed whole villages from the haunting fear of lion-sorcerers and magic leopards. Years of trekking and stalking, endless patience, risks calculated and taken: all these intermingled against a background of wild life, the boundless bush, and the constellations of the African night. Here were some of the pictures, I thought, which must be passing through Bullit's memory now. I felt quite sure of it when he said, as though in a dream: "Kihoro remembers those days."

The sound of his own voice brought him back to present-day realities: but not entirely, since he then exclaimed: "How is such a thing possible?" Seeing that I had failed to grasp what his question referred to, he went on impatiently: "It's very simple really. If you want to shoot wild animals skillfully, you have to understand them through and through. In order to understand them, you have to love them; and the greater your love, the more of them you kill. In fact it's even worse than that in practice. The degree of your love is an exact indication of your need to kill, and the pleasure you derive from the act. After that it makes no difference whether you go hungry or not, or whether you show a profit or a loss. With or without a license, in scheduled or forbidden territory, in pursuit of a dangerous carnivore or some harmless bush buck, it's all one. If your intended victim possesses beauty, nobility, or charm—if he stirs you to the depths of your heart by his strength and gracefulness—then you kill, kill, kill. Why? For God's sake—*why?*"

"I don't know," I said. "Perhaps the moment before you fire is the only time you can feel that the beast truly belongs to you."

"Perhaps," Bullit said, and shrugged.

A herd of gazelle passed across the middle of the clearing, against the backdrop of Kilimanjaro. Their slender horns, swept back almost horizontally, curved with the graceful symmetry of a wing in flight.

Bullit watched them go. Then he said: "Today it makes my heart glad to look at them. Just to look at them. But in the old days I would have picked out the biggest, fastest buck, with the finest coat—and I wouldn't have missed."

"Was it your marriage that changed you?" I asked.

"No. It happened before I'd even met Sybil. I'm not sure if I can even explain it very well. One day you fire, and the animal goes down in the usual way; but you suddenly realize that the victory leaves you quite indifferent. That strongest of all emotions—the blood lust, whatever you like to call it—simply isn't there any more." Bullit ran one large hand through the thick red mat of hair that covered his chest. "You go on out of sheer habit till the day comes when you can't go on any longer. Your love for these wild beasts has changed. Now you want to watch them live, not make them die."

Bullit walked to the veranda steps, and stood looking out over the vast landscape, all shimmering now with heat haze.

"I'm not the only case," he said. "Every Warden of a National Park is a former professional hunter, a converted

◇◇

killer, you might say." He smiled mirthlessly. "But just as I was a more successful and ruthless killer than the rest of them, so now I've gone further than they have to the other extreme. Question of temperament, I suppose. And be-sides—"

Bullit left his sentence hanging in mid-air. Then he turned his gaze toward the far end of the clearing, where the pool now seemed a mere pewter-gray mirror to the sunlight.

"Is that where Patricia—joined the beasts?" he asked.

"Indeed it is. I wouldn't have believed it if I hadn't seen it with my own eyes."

Bullit said: "When your intentions toward them are wholly innocent, the beasts know it."

He turned to face me, and seemed (as had struck me several times before) to be searching my features for some explanatory sign which he could not discover.

At last he said: "Kihoro informed me that you and the child had a long talk together."

"Patricia was very friendly, affectionate even," I told him. "At least, she was till she remembered that I was leaving tomorrow. From that moment I was no longer her friend."

"Yes," Bullit said softly. "I can understand that."

He shut his eyes. His shoulders slumped brokenly, and his arms hung limp. He looked like some great sick animal himself. "She has to feel absolutely alone," he murmured. Then he blinked his eyes open and said: "Are you *really* sure you can't stay a little longer?"

I said nothing.

"We have a radio link with Nairobi every morning and

evening," Bullit insisted. There was a humble, almost beseeching note in his voice. "You could get them to change the date of your booking."

I said nothing.

"I suppose everyone has their various duties in this life," Bullit said, finally. Then he went without a glance in my direction, just as Patricia had done.

❁

10

I left the veranda and went inside for lunch. The steep, pointed roof of thatch and the thick mud-plastered walls combined to produce at least a sensation of coolness. Bogo had opened some tins and a bottle of beer. I asked him if he had seen Patricia again. He said "No, sah," and relapsed into silence. Knowing him as I did, I had hardly hoped for anything else. Nevertheless, the tiny geometrical figures into which the countless wrinkles on his cheeks and forehead naturally fell—triangles, squares, circles—were now working in a strange fashion.

He went on, as though despite himself: "I not seen the little white girl again. But everyone hereabouts in the village talk to me 'bout her."

Bogo broke off, hesitating. I pretended to be absorbed in my food. Any question might scare him off the subject for good. It was surprising enough that he wanted to talk about it at all.

"Folks," Bogo said, "love her, love her very much. But she scare them."

"She *scares* them?" I exclaimed.

"She bewitch the animals," Bogo said, lowering his voice. "She sorceress. Someone swear to me, her Daddy a lion."

Thinking of Bullit's face, I said: "What are they really trying to say? That her father is *like* a lion?"

"No, sah," Bogo corrected me. "These folk mean a real lion."

His voice had lost much of its usual neutrality, and the rucked, squamous skin that covered his face had turned from black to a dirty gray, as though fear had drained the pigmentation out of it. And yet Bogo was a Christian, dressed in European clothes, and read English-language Kenya newspapers.

"Do you really believe that's possible?" I asked him.

"Everything possible, sah," my driver whispered. "Everything, if God will it."

What was he thinking of? The God of the missionaries, or those other hoary powers, rooted for countless centuries in the dark soil of Africa?

Softly he went on: "People seen this little girl in the bush, lying down 'longside a great lion, and the lion, he hold her between his front paws like she was his own baby."

"Who's seen that?" I asked.

"Folk," Bogo answered. "People."

"What people?"

"Folk who seen it. Folk who know," Bogo said, and stared at me unhappily. I couldn't make up my mind if he wanted me to share his fear, or hold myself superior to it.

"Come now, Bogo," I said. "Think of all the travelers' tales we've heard on this trip, that you've translated for me! In Uganda people had seen panther-men. In Tanganyika it was snake-men. On Lake Victoria there were even some people who'd talked to Lutembe, the great crocodile god: and he's a thousand years old if he's a day."

"That quite right, sah," Bogo said.

Had I convinced him? His voice was once more completely neutral. His features had returned to their habitual inscrutability.

A ranger came into the bungalow, and Bogo translated his message. This ranger, he said, was at my disposal for the remainder of my visit. Besides, regulations demanded it. It was forbidden to go anywhere in the National Park unless escorted by an armed guard.

The ranger got into our car, rifle and all, and sat down in the front seat beside Bogo. I retired to the back.

The Reserve was a vast area, stretching on for mile upon mile: scrub gave place to woodland, woodland to open savannah, with occasional hills and mountain peaks. Always in the background, the colossal massif of Kilimanjaro brooded, crowned with snow, keeping watch over the wild, burning lands far below. Everywhere, too, there was wild life visible in abundance. I had never seen so many zebras and ostriches, gazelles and antelopes, such enormous herds of buffalo or such prolific families of giraffes.

There was no fence or hedge or visible mark of any kind to separate the Reserve from the ordinary bush outside. Its boundaries could only be traced on maps or surveys. Yet the animals seemed instinctively aware of this frontier. They appeared to know—and to pass on the knowledge by some mysterious language of their own—that here was their land of refuge, their sanctuary.

At first the magnificent scenery and sheer profusion of

animal life held me entranced. But after a very short time I found that it was just this breathtaking perfection which was responsible for my growing feeling of irritation, even of active resentment. Every time I stopped the car and tried to get close to the animals, on foot, the ranger restricted my movements to a few yards on either side of the track, and still kept at my side like a shadow. If I wanted the car to follow one of the innumerable tracks that wandered away into the woods or hills, toward the shadow of the jungle with its teeming lairs, the ranger would forbid it. We had no authority to deviate in the slightest degree from the official, legal itinerary. This followed a large highway which ran the entire length of the Reserve, and from which one or two side-lanes (constructed by Bullit) occasionally branched off. I remembered the scathing comments he had made to me about tourists, and the precautions he took to ensure that they were kept out of trouble. I was one of them, it seemed: neither more nor less.

If this day of mine in the Reserve had been passed in the normal fashion, as most visitors spent it, I should doubtless have been very happy to contemplate its splendors from the prescribed viewpoint. But Bullit had promised to show me all its secret sanctuaries; and, above all, I had watched at the pool at dawn, with Patricia beside me.

From time to time the ranger would point a long, black, bony hand to right or left and say *"Simba"* or *"Tembo."* These words—the only ones I knew in his language— meant that in some distant, thorny thicket (where I was forbidden to go) lions had their den; or that over on the other side (out of sight behind those low volcanic hills which were out of bounds for me) herds of elephant roamed. And still my car sped on down the official road. I had the feeling of being punished, deprived, frustrated, cheated of my due. Finally, heat and dust helped to break down my will power. I couldn't stand it any longer, and told Bogo to turn round and drive back to camp.

Outside my bungalow the ranger came to attention, snapping his black naked heels together and flicking up one black bony hand to his khaki tarboosh in a smart salute. Then he slung his rifle over his shoulder and strolled off toward the native village. The smile he flashed me as he went was as brilliant as his flat, polished brass buttons. He had accomplished his mission: to protect me from the animals—and from myself.

I glanced up at the sun. I still had an hour or so to spare before going over to Bullit's bungalow for tea. What was to be done with this time?

The heat haze was now completely gone: the sky was a pure, lucid transparency. Light and shade had renewed their checkered patterns on the ground and against the great sweep of the mountain. On its flat, lopped-off summit—a fantastic white marble slab, like some altar made ready for a cosmic sacrifice—the motionless, eternal snow was now coming to life. Its surface foamed and glowed mysteriously, as though it were a great breaking wave, whose crest and trough flickered with changing lights: orange and vermilion, pearl-gray and gold.

There were no beasts now at the far end of the clearing. The birds were silent, and the monkeys had stopped their chattering. Not a bough or a leaf stirred among the trees; not a single thorn crackled along the bush tracks. It was the moment of silence, rest, and intermission, now charged with all its solemn powers. Dusk had not yet fallen, yet an anticipation of darkness hung in the air. The sun seemed to hang suspended and motionless, before handing over the world with all its creatures to the spreading wings of night.

"What orders, sah?" Bogo asked me.

It was not the actual sound of his voice that made me shiver, but the fact that it brought me back to immediate reality—to the presence, as it were, of my physical self. A moment before there had been some fraction of time —a minute, a second, perhaps only a part of a second— during which I ceased to exist in the miserable, restrictive dimensions of human life. I had been lost utterly in a boundless universe: I and the universe were one.

But Bogo had spoken, and instantly I found myself solidified, scaled down to my physiological elements: it was as though I had been sewn back into my skin against my will. And worse than that: I was compelled to issue orders, to act, to *do* something. What was there I could do that would be in harmony with the bush and the African snows as evening enfolded them?

Out of the cover of the scrub emerged two men. Two Masai.

11

I knew they were Masai the instant I saw them, despite my lack of experience. A traveler may easily become confused between Jalluos, Embu, Wakamba, Kikuyu, Meru, Kipsigui, and many of the other native tribes that inhabit

Kenya. But if, in his wanderings through the great parched plains and torrid bush country, he has ever run into a group of Masai—one encounter would be quite sufficient—he will never forget them, or mistake them for anyone else.

These two had the characteristic gait, indolent yet springy: they walked like princes. They had that superb poise of the head, that special way of carrying their spears and the drape of cloth they wore over one shoulder, which at one and the same time covered their body and revealed its splendid nakedness. They had the mysterious beauty which they had inherited from their ancestors, black men who had migrated from the Nile by unknown routes untold centuries ago. Their features and movements alike betrayed a strange bravura, extravagant and inspired. Above all there was a quality of freedom about them— the proud, absolute, indescribable freedom of a people who envy no man or race on earth. Their heritage is poor enough in material terms: a few poor head of cattle, the primitive weapons they make from the ore they find in the dry river beds. These fulfill all their needs. Their pride is so intense that they never leave either house or grave on the face of the earth.

The two Masai who had just appeared now skirted round the edge of the compound. They held their heads high and straight, and both moved at the same quick, light, easy pace. Yet one of them was an old man, and the other a *morane*. This means that he belonged to a special age-group, defined by ancient tribal custom. When the young warriors emerge from their period of adolescence to become their family's pride and the chosen elite of the clan, they have no other duties for a period of years except to be courageous and handsome—and to display these attributes in public. The special distinguishing mark of this privileged group is their bushy hair.

Now most of the natives in East Africa, men and women alike, keep their heads clean-shaven from childhood to the grave. The *moranes* are the only exception to this rule. For the whole of their young adult life in the tribe, they never so much as touch their thick kinky hair with razor or scissors. For this reason, as soon as it has grown well down over their forehead, they devote much time and ingenuity to its adornment. They rub it with the sap of a certain plant, the effect of which is to induce a quicker and stronger growth. They plait it in fine ropes no thicker than a strand of liana, and then interweave the plaits themselves till they form a solid, crimped mass. This they rub daily with cow's fat, till it acquires a shining, lacquered surface without a chink anywhere. Finally they coat it over with a layer of clay and red mud. By this time it is no mere head of hair that these young men so proudly display, but a unique, outlandish *thing*—a cross between a nest of tawny, petrified serpents, a burning bush, and a bronze helmet, with its pointed beaver overshadowing a pair of savage eyebrows in front, and curving down behind onto its owner's ebony neck.

The old man and the *morane* were coming toward my hut. I told Bogo to ask them to stop for a moment.

"But sah—b-but—" Bogo stammered. His face under its network of wrinkles had gone papery gray.

"But these are *Masai*," he concluded, wretchedly.

Bogo himself was a Kikuyu. He remembered only too

well how the Masai—those herdsmen of the bare savannahs, those rootless, merciless nomads, those born warriors—had for long centuries razed, burned, and exterminated the villages of his more sedentary tribe. It was
true that the English had put a stop to the slaughtering of
Kikuyu; but a few peaceful years were not enough to wipe
out such archetypal terrors from the victims' minds.

"I am here with you," I said to Bogo, gently. "And the
rangers with their rifles aren't too far away."

"That's true, sah," Bogo muttered. But when he spoke
to the Masai, his voice was completely toneless.

"*Kouahéri,*" he said, which was clearly a conventional
form of greeting.

The eyes of the two Masai, standing there black and
naked under the robes draped from their shoulders,
merely glanced at this other black man who dressed
like a European. But Bogo's wrinkled skin became even
ashier gray than before. Their expression conveyed a degree of contempt little short of sheer disgust. It was the
way you might look at a caterpillar before squashing it
underfoot and forgetting it. Bogo might have adapted himself to new customs, but the Masai never changed.

"*Kouahéri,*" I said, in my turn.

The *morane* waited to see what line the old man would
take. The old man's eyes met mine: he stared hard at me,
summing me up. Obviously I was not his equal. No other
race on earth could, man for man, match the Masai. On
the other hand I was a white, and thus a stranger on this
earth, a distinguished visitor. Politeness to me would in-
volve no loss of face.

"*Kouahéri,*" the old man said, graciously if with a certain *hauteur*.

◇◇◇

"*Kouahéri,*" said the *morane*. Both his voice and face remained totally devoid of expression.

The old man now planted his tall spear in the ground before him. One sharp thrust was enough. Then he stood there waiting, as straight and erect as the spear itself. The *morane*, who had kept his spear at his side, now leaned on it, holding it with both hands. This movement bent his neck and torso into a shallow arc. Was he, I wondered, trying to show me that even when an aged Masai chief felt obliged to behave courteously, his own privileged position permitted—demanded, even—that he should remain insolently aloof? Or did he know instinctively that the pose he had adopted was the one best calculated to show off his astounding good looks?

His youthful body resembled that of some athletic Greek warrior just emerged from adolescence. Under the black, lustrous skin rippled muscles which, for all their fine-drawn delicacy, were enormously powerful. Nothing could better emphasize his strength, vitality, and sheer animal beauty than this slight, nonchalant twist of the body. His face seemed lit from within by a glowing, golden fire; his mouth was strong, his nose straight and firm, while his great eyes, bright with indolence, yet contained a glint of fiery savageness in their still depths. Crowning everything was the great dressed mass of hair, like burnished copper. His whole head, resting on one naked black half-bent arm, blended in its expression a relaxed, sleepy tenderness and the cruelty of a primitive mask.

Such vigorous, youthful beauty, now in its first and finest flower, could break every rule made for lesser mortals: this was no less than its due. The *morane* stood there, awaiting our admiration, as fierce, subtle, and innocent as a black panther that sprawls in the sun, stretching out his sleek, velvety, murderer's paws. What more could one ask of him?

I made Bogo ask him his name. The *morane* himself contemptuously kept silent; it was the old man who answered for him.

He said: "His name is Oriunga." Then he added: "And I am called Ol'Kalu."

Then he asked me a brief question, which Bogo translated.

"He want to know, sah, why you here."

"Tell him, because of the wild animals."

Ol'Kalu spoke again. "He don't understand," Bogo interpreted. "He say, no one can kill animals here. Then why you come?"

There was a silence at this. Then I asked what the two Masai were doing in the Reserve themselves.

Ol'Kalu said: "We are searching for grazing-land for our herds, and a place for our families to camp."

His cheek resting on one arm, and the arm itself propped against his spear, the *morane* stood there staring at me through long, drooping eyelashes. His stance conveyed a fascinating impression of lazy arrogance.

Silence fell once more; but this time I could think of nothing further to say. The aged Masai raised one hand in a gesture of farewell. This movement dislodged the cloth draped over his shoulder; it fell away, leaving his whole body exposed, and revealing a gigantic furrowed scar that ran down his lean, scrawny torso from neck to groin. This horrible cicatrice, with its puckered ridges and deep, sunken pits of scar tissue, had the tint and texture of cured meat or dry, clotted blood.

Ol'Kalu, seeing me stare at it, remarked: "The hide of even the best-made shield cannot stand up to a lion's claws."

The old man plucked his spear from the ground and examined it thoughtfully. It was long and heavy, yet beautifully balanced. Sharpened at both ends, and equipped halfway down the shaft with a cylindrical metal hilt designed to fit its warrior-owner's grasp, it could equally well serve as throwing-spear or javelin. Ol'Kalu shook this spear in one hand, while the fingers of the other traced the course of his frightful scar. He said: "Those were the days when the whites did not interfere with the *moranes'* amusements."

Oriunga opened his sleepy eyes under their coppery-golden helmet of hair, and smiled. His teeth were regular, pointed, and as white as any carnivore's.

Obey the white man if you like, this pitiless smile seemed to say. It is a long time since you were a *morane*. But I am one now, in all my courage and pride. The only law I recognize is my own desire.

The two Masai moved off, their gait as indolent and springy as ever. From a distance their figures displayed, in silhouette, a precision of line and gracefulness of movement which—together with the spears they carried—suggested a resemblance to the hunters in a prehistoric cave painting.

"What orders, sah?" Bogo asked me.

But there was nothing left for me to do in this place, where men were more alien and secretive and inaccessible than the wild beasts themselves.

"Go and pack," I told him. "We're leaving first thing tomorrow."

❀

12

There was only one thing that impelled me to accept Sybil Bullit's pressing invitation: the thought of seeing Patricia again. But when I arrived at the bungalow, Patricia was not there.

"Ah, well," Sybil said, "it's still light. Patricia very seldom gets home before sundown." Then she gave a nervous laugh and added, as though in explanation: "You see, she's got a poetic streak."

She was wearing high-heeled shoes and a flowered silk dress cut very low both in front and behind. Round her neck hung a string of pearls. She was, in fact, rather overdressed for such an informal occasion; and in the same way both her scent and make-up were a little too much in evidence.

Her voice and bearing had undergone a similar transformation. They weren't exactly artificial or affected; but they carried something of that half-factitious animation and brisk, commanding gaiety of manner by which a hostess suggests that she is determined both to sparkle herself and make her guests sparkle too. Her voice was pitched just a shade higher than usual, and her gestures were very slightly more flamboyant.

Such painstaking preparations, and all for the sake of a passing stranger! It was plain that loneliness had sharpened Sybil's need for social life to an extraordinary degree if the mere fact of my presence could produce such feverish excitement in her. The dark glasses, too, had disappeared.

Bullit was wearing a white drill suit, carefully starched and pressed, with a club tie. His unruly hair had been combed out and plastered down on his skull with water—which only served to emphasize more strongly the heavy animal coarseness of his features. He appeared sullen and ill at ease.

"Relax," he said to me. "Patricia'll be here soon enough."

I had not so much as mentioned Patricia's name, or shown in any way how disappointed I was by her absence. Yet now they both began discussing her at once. I felt as though they were taking advantage of my presence to resume a conversation begun before I arrived.

"Well, anyhow," Sybil said brightly, "there's no point in holding up tea for our little bush-ranger, is there?" Her laughter had the same forced, artificial quality I had noticed when she first welcomed me.

We moved through from the drawing-room to the dining-room. Here were laid out all those accessories so essential for a formal tea party in any upper-class English home. The teapot, milk jug, hot water jug, and sugar bowl were all of antique silver. The plates and cups were early Wedgwood. There were lace table mats and embroidered napkins; the table itself was loaded with milk, saucers of sliced lemon, buttered toast, cakes, strawberry jam, tiny cheese sandwiches, and heaven knows what else. In the middle stood a big cut-glass flower vase, full of pinks, pansies, and anemones—in fact, those same colorless, fragile European blooms over which I had watched Sybil agonize in lonely despair.

"I don't know how to thank you for giving me this wonderful welcome," I said to her.

"Oh, *please!* I'm only too delighted to have an excuse to get out the few decent things we possess. And the food's too easy—straight out of tins, most of it." She gave another of her awkward laughs—they seemed to have all been saved up for our second meeting—and then, seeing me look at the flower vase, stopped abruptly and said: "Ah. You were talking about my flowers, were you?" For the first time that afternoon her voice was both serious and sincere; she had dropped her pitch noticeably, and now spoke at an ordinary speed. Her eyes, too, had lost the expression of ostentatious pride with which she had displayed her possessions, and recaptured that breathtaking loveliness I had glimpsed in them, for brief moments, during the morning.

"We might as well sit down," Bullit said.

Two native houseboys in white uniform—baggy trousers gathered in at the ankles, long tunics, and purple cummerbunds—now drew up chairs for us. One of them remained empty.

Sybil's head turned toward the window and back again so quickly that I might not have noticed it if Bullit hadn't said, at the same moment, with all the tenderness of which he was capable: "Darling, you can see perfectly well that it's still light."

"Not for long," Sybil murmured. Her eyes were fixed on the empty chair.

"Darling," Bullit repeated, with a quick, embarrassed laugh, "I think our guest might like some tea."

Sybil shivered, straightened herself, and put a hand up to her pearls. I don't think she was aware of this gesture.

Then she smiled and said to me: "How many lumps of sugar do you take? And would you rather have milk or lemon?"

Once again the voice and the smile had become a little exaggerated and artificial. Sybil was slipping back into her role as hostess, which, quite obviously, still gave her considerable satisfaction.

"The cake is excellent," she said. "I have it specially sent out from London—and the jam as well. Do please help yourself. I'm sure you won't have any sort of a proper dinner—men who travel alone are always the same."

She rattled on in this way while filling Bullit's cup and her own. Then, in order to prevent the conversation getting one-sided, and to bring her guest into the picture, she asked me what impression I had formed of the Reserve during my conducted trip.

"The scenery is wonderful," I said. "And I saw a great many animals—from a distance." As I said this I glanced covertly at Bullit; but he was staring out through the window at the lengthening evening shadows.

"Oh, but that's the best way to look at them," Sybil exclaimed. "All animals look nicest at long range. Especially gazelles. You know, we've got a tame one here, an adorable little creature—"

"I know Cymbeline," I told her. "We're good friends."

"John," Sybil said to her husband, "you ought to tell our friend—"

Her voice trailed away; Bullit was still staring out of the window. Sybil gave a sharp order to the native houseboys. One of them went and drew the curtains, while the other switched on the electric light.

"*No!*" Sybil cried out. She made as though to put on her

dark glasses, realized that she didn't have them, and shaded her eyes with one hand instead.

"The candles, John, *please*," she said impatiently.

There were two large antique silver candlesticks standing on a side table. Bullit lit the candles, and a soft, flickering glow of yellow light suffused the room, playing over the polished silverware and translucent china, picking out the dying flowers and faded blue curtains. Was it true— was it even possible—that immediately outside this isolated room, which seemed at once refuge and illusion, lay the bush, the domain of wild beasts and savages? I thought of old Ol'Kalu and the *morane*, Oriunga.

"Two Masai stopped outside my bungalow today," I said. "I thought they looked quite superb—the young one especially. He was—"

"Stop it, *please!*" Sybil cried. "For God's sake don't go on about them!"

Her role as hostess was forgotten; a hysterical note had crept into her voice. It was as though I had suddenly brought those two barbaric warriors into the room itself; as though they stood there against the blue curtains, lit by soft candle flames.

"I know them," she went on, clutching her temples with both hands. "I know them too well. Their naked, serpentine bodies, their fantastic hair, that mad look in their eyes— And now they're back again."

The window was completely curtained; yet Sybil still glanced toward it in a terrified way, and whispered: "What is to become of me? This place is hell on earth."

Bullit got up abruptly. What was he going to do? It seemed he did not know himself. There he stood, a huge, dumb, clumsy, motionless figure, crammed into Sunday clothes eminently ill-suited to his gigantic frame, strait-jacketed with starch like a limed bird. Under his damp, plastered-down hair he wore the shattering expression of a man who has been wrongly condemned to death, and has no notion why.

Sybil saw what he was undergoing; and the strength of her love for him enabled her to guess the rest. She went quickly round the table, took his hand, and said: "Darling, I'm sorry. I'm all on edge. There's no possible reason for it except Patricia. I know very well that this is the only life for you, ever."

Bullit slowly sat down again, as though a spell had been lifted from him. Sybil went back to her place. On the surface, everything was all right once more. The entertainment game could now be resumed—indeed, should be, without delay.

"John," Sybil said, in the special voice which the game required her to assume, "why don't you tell our guest about some of your safaris? I'm sure he'd find them most interesting. You've had some extraordinary experiences, after all."

"Of course, I'd be only too glad." He would have done anything for Sybil after what Sybil had just done for him. But happiness no less than suffering can put things out of one's mind. Bullit tried to run one hand through his hair, but pulled it back sharply as though he'd been burned when he touched the unfamiliar damp and flattened surface. He said: "I don't know how to begin."

"Why not tell him the story you told me that first evening we met each other?"

◇◇

"Perfect," Bullit said. "Just the thing." He turned to me and began: "It happened in Serenguetti country, about twelve years ago—"

The tale unfolded easily enough. It concerned the hunting of a family of man-eating lions—creatures of exceptional ferocity and quite diabolical cunning. Bullit told it well and simply. Furthermore, there was a special overtone of emotion in what he said: he might ostensibly be addressing me, but his real audience was Sybil. At first, as a good hostess should be, she was exclusively concerned with the effect the story was having on me; but very soon her attention wandered. Her hands and features relaxed, and her face took on that quality of translucent innocence which so enhanced its beauty. It was not this Bullit, entertaining a guest with his reminiscences, whom Sybil now saw and heard, but Bullit as he had been ten years ago—less weighty in the body, his face leaner and more enthusiastic, without the hoarse edge to his voice or the red veins in his eyes. Hers was the Bullit she knew at first meeting; a shy giant who carried the smell of the bush with him, and was haloed with the dangers he had run— Bullit the great white hunter at the height of his fame. And Bullit, for his part, was telling his story for a young girl fresh out from home: a happy, innocent, enchanted creature who sat with him on the flower-heavy veranda of the Norfolk Hotel, or in the bar of the Stanley, or the lounge of the Muthaiga Club, and listened to his tales as no one had ever listened to them before. Who looked into his eyes as no one else had ever done.

Occasionally Sybil would whisper to her husband, jogging his memory, reminding him of a detail omitted here, some incident treated too briefly there. These details and incidents were always designed to emphasize the strength, cruelty, and intelligence of the beasts—and, by implication, Bullit's own courage and professional skill. Thus led on and encouraged by his wife, Bullit recovered his taste for blood; once again he was the famous hunter, the terror of the bush. But the story of his exhausting adventures, the perils of the chase, the paths hacked through thorny jungle, the conferences with naked black trackers, the dangerous and wearing vigils in concealed hides—all this contained, for Sybil and her husband, the enchanting tenderness of lovers' language. And the love it enshrined still lived on.

Suddenly Bullit broke off in mid-sentence. Sybil sat up with an abrupt movement, her face waxy pale. A frightful, prolonged clamor, half roar, half lament, had broken out in the bush, and echoed, reverberating, through the room in which we sat, to a slow dying fall. It might have come from miles away or the immediate vicinity: we could not tell. While it lasted not one of us moved an inch. As soon as silence returned, Sybil ran to the window and threw back the curtains. The sun had set, and the brief dusk was drawing to its close. Shadows marched swiftly across the ground.

"John, John!" Sybil exclaimed. "It's getting dark—"

Bullit went over and joined her. "Not yet, darling," he said. "Not quite."

"But Patricia's never stayed out so late before, never. And night's coming on, it's getting dark—"

Sybil turned back abruptly into the room. She could not bear to stand there and watch the darkness creep up, spreading and thickening like black smoke. The first evening breeze blew in through the open window, and the candle flames flickered.

"John, for God's sake *do* something! Take out the houseboys—alert the rangers—but find Patricia!"

The deep, rumbling growl we had heard a little earlier now broke out again. This time it was fainter and farther off; but still clear enough to inspire terror. Sybil clapped her hands to her ears. Bullit drew the curtains again and shut out the black rising tide of night.

"*Please,* John—"

"All right," Bullit said. "I'll go."

It was at this moment that the door opened, as though of its own volition. Kihoro took one step into the room—a black, scarred, crippled, one-eyed apparition—and stood there without saying a word. Then he winked his one good eye at Bullit, and opened his mouth in a toothless grin. This done, he disappeared once more.

With a thin, keening cry of relief that sounded almost like a sob, Sybil collapsed in an armchair. Bullit ran one huge hand across his forehead. He was deathly white.

"You see, darling," he said, in a low voice, "everything's quite all right."

"Yes," Sybil said. Her face was drained and vacant. Her eyes flickered over the table, with its embroidered napkins, lace mats, Wedgwood china, and antique silver spirit lamp, over which the water was still boiling away. Her strength came back to her, and she said: "Be a lamb, John, and see if you can find Patricia. The poor child must want her tea."

❈

13

When Sybil and I were left alone, she made an obvious effort to put on her "social" voice and manner again. But the shock had been too violent for her.

"I simply don't know what I'm doing any more," she said, shaking her head weakly. "John's always right, of course. But I can't stand it any longer. My nerves are worn out. We've been living like this far too long."

She seemed to think—I don't know why—that I wanted to interrupt at this point, and gestured impatiently with one hand.

"I know, I know. You think it's wonderful here. Of course you would—for a few days. You're just a visitor. You're not in the game yourself. Make this your life and you'll see what I mean. Oh, for the first few months I was the same. I went everywhere with John. The whole place was packed with beauty and charm and adventure and poetry for me. And then, little by little, *it* began—"

She had no need to name the sensation she was alluding to; one glance at her face was enough. It was terror.

In a flat, monotonous voice Sybil recounted each step in her progress toward this ghastly predicament. Once, after the rains, Bullit's Land Rover had bogged down in thick mud, and they were forced to spend the night out in one of the wildest parts of the bush. On another occasion, just after they stopped, a rhinoceros—till that moment hidden in the dense scrub—suddenly charged their car. Only Bullit's lightning reflexes and great skill as a driver had saved them. Another time, in the middle of the night, an elephant had come so close to their caravan (this had been their first home, Sybil told me) that she could hear its breathing, and its heavy tread.

"If that elephant had taken the idea into his head," Sybil said, "he could have overturned that caravan and battered us to death. John's strength and bravery would have been quite useless. Patricia had already arrived then, too, and she was still a baby. It was then I learned what real fear was. It invaded the marrow of my bones. It struck at my very soul. This was not the kind of fear that goes away after a while. Never. This is something different. It gnaws away at you, growing and spreading the whole time. It's the beginning of the end."

Sybil could no longer sleep at night; she lay awake, rigid with terror, listening to every sound in the bush. During the day, while Bullit was driving round the Reserve, devoting all his attention to his precious animals— there was real loathing in Sybil's voice as she said this— she was left at home, alone with the native servants.

"I can't stand them any longer," she suddenly burst out. "Their barbarian laughter, those frightful gleaming white teeth, all their tales of ghosts and panther-men and sorcerers—horrible! And the worst, easily the worst thing of the lot—that trick they have of appearing without you hearing them."

It was at this moment that Bullit returned with Patricia.

I had been waiting all day to see this little girl again with such impatience, such mixed and violent emotions that, more than once, I felt a little ridiculous. Now, here she was before me, in the flesh, and yet I could not rekindle any of the extraordinary feeling she had earlier aroused in me. Besides, what connection was there between that dawn apparition who walked among wild beasts as a friend, and the model child whose hand Bullit now held?

Patricia was wearing a starched sky-blue frock with white collar and cuffs, and a skirt which came a little below her knees. On her feet she wore white socks and little patent-leather shoes. Her modest, shy demeanor matched this outfit very well. She held her slender neck very straight and sensible in its white collar, and her bowl-shaped fringe was combed out evenly above her downcast eyes. She gave me the ghost of a curtsy, kissed her mother, and sat down in the chair we had left for her. The only part of her I recognized as familiar were her hands—especially against the tablecloth: brown, scratched, the nails broken and jagged and each rimmed with an apparently indelible circle of dirt.

Patricia glanced at the array of cakes and jams laid out on the table and said, with sober satisfaction: "What a whopping tea!" She filled her own cup, and took a large slice of cake. Her table manners were perfect, but she kept her eyes obstinately on the floor as she ate.

"Well," Sybil said, "you've seen our young lady at last, so you'll be able to describe her to Lise."

She was, I felt, proud of Patricia; also, she was gradually regaining her self-possession.

"You know," she announced brightly to Patricia, "our guest is a friend of Lise Darbois."

Patricia remained silent.

"You remember Lise, don't you? I've often talked about her."

"Yes, Mummy, I remember," Patricia said, without raising her eyes. Her clear, well-modulated voice did not recall in any particular that secretive way of speech she had adopted at our meeting near the pool. It was plain from her present tone that she had no intention of taking part in our conversation; but Sybil was determined to make her daughter shine.

"Don't be so shy, darling," she said. "Tell our friend something about the Reserve, and the animals. You know all about them, don't you?"

"Nothing of the least interest," Patricia said, her neck tense, her eyes fixed steadily on her plate.

"Really, you're *too* uncouth!" Sybil exclaimed, with an uncontrollable flicker of irritation. It looked as though her nerves were beginning to get out of hand again. Then she forced a laugh and said to Bullit: "John, I hope your memory is better than your daughter's. You haven't finished telling us about your big expedition—you know, your Serenguetti story—"

At this point there took place a little scene as brief as it was astonishing. At her mother's final words Patricia did something she had not done since coming into the room: she looked up, very abruptly, and stared straight at Bullit. It was as though he had been expecting this gesture, and dreading it. At first he would not meet her eyes. But Patricia's delicate, mobile face now stiffened, became almost petrified in her effort to beat down Bullit's resistance by sheer will power. Finally she succeeded, and his eyes met hers. Helplessness, guilt, suffering, and supplication mingled in his expression. But Patricia's face remained obdurate.

It was only later that I grasped the true significance of

this silent exchange; but it was very clear to Sybil. Her lips went white, and she trembled uncontrollably. She said, her voice rising higher with each word she uttered: "Well, John, I see you've gone as dumb as your daughter. You always gang up against me, the pair of you, don't you? You haven't even reproached her for coming home at all hours and nearly killing me with anxiety—have you? Have you?"

"Believe me, Mummy, I'm sorry," Patricia said. "Really sorry. But King was very late today, and he absolutely insisted on seeing me home. You heard him, I suppose."

"Of course," Bullit said. "His call is quite unmistakable—"

Sybil cut through her husband's remarks, effectively silencing him. "Stop it, stop it," she cried. "I won't—I can't live in this crazy atmosphere another minute—" She turned toward me, convulsed by a silent, senseless fit of laughter, a kind of dumb hysteria, and shouted: "Do you know who this 'King' is that my daughter waits for till evening, and who sees her home, and whose call my husband recognizes? Do you know?"

She drew a deep, gulping breath and shrieked: "A lion! A *lion,* I tell you! A wild beast. A carnivorous monster—"

She had reached the brink of a real *crise de nerfs,* and must have realized the fact. The shame and misery she felt at behaving in such a way before a stranger wiped every other emotion off her face. She turned and ran out of the room.

Patricia sat stiffly in her starched frock. The sunburn on her cheeks seemed to have lost its luster.

"Go with her," she told her father. "She needs you."

Bullit obeyed.

Patricia looked at me: her expression was quite unfathomable. I too got up and went out. There was nothing I could do for any of them.

The natives in the Reserve had spoken of Patricia as the lion's child, and it was true.

14

Bogo was waiting for me outside my bungalow. He followed me in and asked when I wanted dinner. His uniform, his voice, his face, his attitude, the necessity of answering his question—all these things irritated me in the most extraordinary way.

"I haven't the faintest idea," I said. "Anyway, it's not important at all. I'll look after it myself, later."

"Sah—you want I pack everything tonight, then we leave early tomorrow," Bogo said.

"We'll leave when I decide to leave," I said, clenching my teeth.

Bogo hesitated a moment, head bent; then he said: "But—but we *do* leave tomorrow, eh, sah? Don't we?"

His tone suggested fear, reproach, and a stubborn determination to leave the Reserve at the first possible moment. I found it quite intolerable.

"That," I told him, "is my business, and no one else's."

"And your plane, sah?" he murmured.

Doubtless I should have acted as I did even if my driver had not shown such obstinacy. But at that moment it seemed to me that my only motive was the natural in-

stinct to rebel against his hateful insistence. I tore a leaf
from my notebook, scribbled a few lines on it, and told
Bogo to take it across to the Bullits' bungalow at once. It
contained a request that Bullit, during the course of his
next transmission to Nairobi by radio link, should cancel
the seat I had reserved on the Zanzibar plane for the
day after tomorrow.

The generator, according to the regulations laid down
for the Reserve, closed down at ten o'clock. I lit the hurricane lamp and sat down on the veranda. The whisky stood
at my elbow, but I did not touch it. I no more wanted a
drink than I did food or sleep; or, indeed, time to think
and reflect. It was cool, and the night sky was clear.
Through the darkness I could just make out the sharp
lines of the thorn bushes and the table-top of Kilimanjaro.
The mud-and-thatch veranda roof hid the constellations
and the heaven above me; it did not matter. My thoughts
were utterly practical, utterly trivial. I was wondering if
I had omitted anything vital from the shopping-list I had
given Bogo. He was to go off at sunrise to a village called
Laitokito, about twenty-five miles outside the Reserve, to
buy fresh provisions from the Indian storekeeper there. I
recalled, with some amusement, how terrified my old
tortoise of a driver had been to learn that our stay among
the wild beasts was to be prolonged indefinitely. After that
I thought about nothing at all. No doubt I was tired.

The countless small noises of the bush—crackling
twigs, tiny whispers and whickerings and sighs—rose all
round the bungalow, like some secret nocturnal language.
Occasionally a louder sound rose above the endless mur-
muring—a shrill cry, a raucous howl, a sharp-edged

hunting-call. And from time to time huge shadows loomed across the far end of the clearing.

I sat there a long time, my mind blank and inactive. What was the point of forcing myself to think? Someone was sure to come to me, someone who would explain everything—the mysteries of the night, the reason for my journey to the National Park, the reason for my inability to leave it. But it was in vain that I prolonged my vigil. I stayed till the first blush of dawn tinted the veranda rail a faint pink; but no one came, no one at all.

PART TWO

Wearily I blinked my eyes

open. This time it was not an extraordinary little monkey that woke me, but my driver, Bogo.

"Time to eat, sah!" he said. "Time to eat!"

"Breakfast?" I said, vaguely.

"No, sah. Lunch. Is after midday."

I said: "I went to sleep very late."

There was a suggestion of self-excuse in my reply. I had not intended to apologize or explain, but I couldn't help it. For weeks now I had got Bogo accustomed to an extremely strict routine. Our plans were worked out in close detail: times of departure and arrival, meals and daily itinerary, all were dovetailed into a rigid pattern. I had gone to unbelievable lengths in order to cram each moment of my trip with new experiences and sensations; and Bogo had thrown himself wholeheartedly into the job of executing my plans. Now here I was abjuring my own rules, and jettisoning a discipline which had taken much time and trouble to build up. I had to get out of bed and have a meal. The day was half gone already.

My body was stiff and aching. This, I surmised, came of having spent almost the whole night out on the veranda, without budging. I traipsed over to the bath hut.

But neither hot nor cold water could perform their usual small miracle of relaxation on my mind and body. My stiffness was of the moral variety. I was irritated with everything and everybody, myself most of all.

How much longer was I going to condemn myself to this ghastly bread-and-jam *regime*? And what about Zanzibar? There would be no time for me to go there now. Zanzibar, the island paradise of the Indian Ocean, with its warm, balmy, clove-scented air. Anyway, what could I expect to find in the Reserve that would compensate for the loss of the last, and almost certainly the best, part of my journey?

The wild animals, I thought. But if I had to resume the kind of conducted Cook's Tour I had experienced the previous day, with a ranger watching every step I took, I might as well just stay in my bungalow. At least it was protected from the heat and dust, and I could spend my time drinking the case of whisky which Bogo, on my instructions, had brought back from Laitokitok.

Why on earth had I ordered a whole case? Who was it for? Bullit? But Bullit detested me and had made no secret of the fact. As for Sybil, since I had witnessed her *crise de nerfs*, she quite obviously couldn't stand me any longer. And Patricia's resentment had now blazed up into a new, positively poisonous hatred.

All three of them, beyond any doubt, had only one desire as far as I was concerned: to see me a thousand miles away as quickly as possible. Yet here I was putting down roots, clinging to them like a barnacle—just as I had insisted on leaving when they all wanted me to stay.

Every moment I found myself cursing, with increasing vehemence, my obstinate determination to remain in the

Reserve. But at the same time, ever since the decision had been taken, I had refused to recognize its motive. It embarrassed me: the whole thing was too childish and ridiculous for words.

By now I had finished my meal. The food was tasteless and the beer lukewarm.

"What orders, sah?" Bogo asked.

"None," I said, making a great effort to keep calm. "Go and have your siesta."

From the doorway a clear young voice remarked: "No, keep him here. You're going to need him."

It was Patricia. As I might have expected, she had appeared without a sound to warn me of her approach. She was once more dressed in a pair of gray overalls, but a little of the calculated good behavior and carefully learned demureness which she had put on the day before at tea time still clung to her manner now. Nicholas, the little monkey, was perched on her shoulder, and Cymbeline the gazelle walked beside her.

"My father has transmitted your message to Nairobi," Patricia said, "and Mummy wants you to come over for dinner tonight. They were delighted to hear that you're not leaving the Reserve today, after all."

Patricia spaced out the words of this little speech with careful emphasis. Her expression clearly insisted on an equal display of courteous good manners when I made my reply.

I said: "I am most grateful to your parents. What you have just told me gives me great pleasure. And I am delighted to accept their invitation."

"Please accept my thanks on their behalf," said Patricia.

At this moment I realized that my interest in what Bullit or his wife thought of me was negligible. I said: "And what about you, Patricia? Are you glad I'm staying on for a while?"

The change in Patricia's expression was almost imperceptible; but it sufficed to transform her small, sunburned face completely. The features were still seriously composed, indeed; but their gravity was not that of a little girl who has learned good manners. No; this was the subtle, sensitive, alert seriousness that belonged to the child who had surprised me near the pool at the foot of Kilimanjaro. Without any apparent reason, I at once felt fresh hope and happiness surging up in me.

"I wonder why you *are* staying," Patricia said, almost to herself.

It suddenly seemed very easy for me to say what, till this moment, I had refused to admit even to myself.

"Because of King," I told her. "Because of the lion."

Patricia nodded quickly several times, with vigorous approval—a gesture which dislodged the little monkey from her shoulder. Then she said: "Mummy and Daddy never thought of King as an explanation. But *I* knew all right."

"Are we friends again now?" I asked.

Patricia said, quite seriously: "You stayed because of King. It's for him to answer that question, not me."

There was a strange sound at this point from Bogo: something midway between a gasp and a sob. He seemed to be having difficulty in breathing, and his face had turned a queer gray.

"What do you need Bogo for?" I asked Patricia.

"You'll find out later. It's not time yet."

I was suddenly seized by a sort of anxious impatience. These words of Patricia's seemed to hint at a promise, an agreement to be kept between us. She hadn't come simply to bring a message from her parents. This merely served as an excuse for a more important and secret decision. I closed my eyes for a moment as one does to conquer a fit of dizziness. Was it possible that the child's plan was *really* what I suspected?

I pulled myself together. There I went again, slipping into my fantastic, childish dream world. All I had to do now was to wait till the time—Patricia's time—actually came. But I felt I couldn't stay cooped up inside the four walls of the bungalow.

"Come outside," I said to Patricia, and told Bogo to bring me a whisky.

"Have you got any lemonade?" Patricia inquired, bright-eyed.

Bogo and I exchanged glances. It was hard to say which of us was more out of countenance.

"Maybe," Bogo suggested nervously, "maybe Miss like soda water?"

"Yes," said Patricia, "if you give me some sugar and lemons with it. Then I can make lemonade for myself."

She set about mixing this cocktail with great care, her face toward the clearing and the great mountain behind it. At this time of day the sun stripped Kilimanjaro bare of all color and shadow.

"Have you been out with the animals?" I asked.

"No. I had breakfast at the same time as Mummy did, and I've been doing my lessons with her all morning. Everything went very nicely."

Patricia had been blowing on the soda water to make

more bubbles come up. Now she stopped, and said in a quieter voice: "Poor Mummy—she's so happy when I take a little trouble over my work that she forgets everything else. After what happened yesterday evening I simply had to help her. It was my duty."

She began to blow in her glass again, but the gesture was now merely mechanical. The tortured comprehension written all over her face was that of an adult. Life was even more difficult for Patricia than I had supposed. She loved her mother, and was well aware how much she hurt Sybil by her behavior; yet at the same time she could do nothing to remedy the situation short of ceasing to be her individual self.

Patricia stirred her drink with one finger, which she then took out and sucked, running her tongue round the broken nail. She poured a little more sugar into the mixture. "Mummy's very clever," she went on proudly. "She knows all about history and geography and math and grammar. I can learn very fast, too, if I want to."

Her voice, without warning, took on the flat, secretive tone she used to avoid scaring wild game: it was the first time I had heard it since our conversation by the great pool.

"You know," she said, "when I went to school in Nairobi, I saw at once I was well ahead of all the other girls. I could have gone up a form or two right away. But I played stupid to get myself sent home quicker. I'd have died if they'd kept me there."

Patricia glanced eagerly down toward the clearing, her eye lingering on the light-flaked reflections that shimmered off the water into the far distance, pausing at each dense clump of trees as though trying to penetrate to their very heart. Then she gulped down the rest of her lemonade and said: "Tell your driver we're leaving right away."

She took the little monkey off her shoulder and set him down on Cymbeline's back. "Go on, both of you, back to the house," she said. The gazelle, with Nicholas still clinging to her, moved delicately down the veranda steps, and set off in the direction of the Bullits' bungalow. Her hooves were hardly bigger than thimbles, I reflected.

Patricia skipped gaily after her and opened the car door.

"If I was alone," she said, "I'd go on foot, as usual. But since you're coming with me—"

Her big dark eyes sparkled with cheerful mischief. She was obviously picturing how out of breath I would get trying to keep up with her, and how the thorn bushes through which she slipped so adroitly would baffle and tear my clumsy body.

"Where to, Miss?" Bogo asked.

Patricia answered him very rapidly in Kikuyu. He turned toward me, and sheer terror was stamped on every line of his face. Even the whites of his eyes looked glazed.

"Silence, you!" Patricia snapped. "Hold your tongue!"

She had reverted to her own tongue, the natural language in which to issue commands. She had the ingrained, arrogant authority of all children whose black servants have obeyed them unquestioningly from the day they were born.

"But—but, Miss, sah," Bogo stammered. "Is forbidden, is *absolutely* forbidden to go among the animals without ranger along same time—"

"That's true," I said to Patricia. "Your father—"

"When you are with me," the girl exclaimed, "you need no one else to protect you."

While I still hesitated, Kihoro suddenly emerged from behind a thorn bush and came over toward us. He walked with his chest thrust awkwardly out over his broken pelvis, as though the weight of the two-barreled hunting-rifle he carried over one shoulder was crushing him. He stopped quite close to the car and stared at me out of his one good eye. I understood his embarrassment. It was his job to keep an eye on the child when she went out on her expeditions—but without her knowing it. How was he to follow her if she came in the car with me?

"Well," I said, "since we haven't got a ranger, let's take Kihoro as a substitute—"

"As a *substitute*?" Patricia said indignantly. "A *substitute*? He's the best tracker and the finest shot in the whole Reserve. *And* he knows it better than anybody." She paused, then added: "*And* he belongs to *me*."

She beckoned to Kihoro. With a sideways, scuttling movement, like a crab—his crippled body made it impossible for him to walk in any other way—he went and joined Bogo, who gave a little shiver of disgust. There was nothing in common between the smartly uniformed rangers, trained to deal with visitors, and this scarred, one-eyed creature whose clothes stank of sweat and the bush. Worst of all, Kihoro was a Wakamba; and apart from the Masai, the Wakamba were the most cruel and warlike tribe in the whole of Kenya.

We drove off along the main road—the only legitimate route for tourists—with which I was already familiar. Patricia leaned back against one of the elbow rests, stretched her legs out along the seat, crossed and uncrossed them, and half-shut her eyes. "Your car's just like a well-sprung bed on wheels," she observed.

The car was in fact a hired Chevrolet limousine, several years old, it is true, but far bigger and better sprung than Bullit's Land Rover, which was a kind of glorified jeep.

"It only has two disadvantages," Patricia went on, stretching herself with an air of luxurious well-being. "It will never get through where the Land Rover does; and you can't see what's going on outside when you're in it."

She slithered across the seat to my side, shaking with silent laughter, and whispered: "Look at Kihoro—don't you think he's just like a miserable old ape shut up in a cage?"

Though Patricia had spoken as low as she could, the old native tracker had caught the sound of his own name, and turned round in the front seat. I had never seen his mangled features at such close range before. Set among a dozen or more cicatrices, his right eye, deep and black in its socket, resembled some deep wound rimmed with blood.

Patricia gestured negatively to Kihoro, and the scarred face turned back once more to contemplate the road ahead of us.

"How did the poor devil get so horribly marked?" I asked Patricia.

"There's nothing 'poor' about him," she replied, in an assured voice. "Blacks don't feel bad about being ugly. And their hunters are proud of the scars they acquire on safari."

"How did Kihoro—"

"Well," Patricia said, "he didn't break his pelvis or get

that crippled shoulder out hunting. Both those accidents happened to him in the Reserve—and both because he over-estimated his ability to deal with wild animals. The first time it was a buffalo: he was tossed and gored. The second, he was squashed, against the trunk of a tree he was trying to climb, by a charging rhino."

"But his *face*," I persisted. "Surely those are claw marks."

"There's no mistaking them, is there?" Patricia said. I looked at her more closely: both face and voice had betrayed an odd flicker of pride as she uttered these words. All the time she told the story her eyes grew darker, her mouth more animated.

The claws which had furrowed their way through Kihoro's face belonged to a leopard. Kihoro had stalked him a long time, with the single cartridge in his gun which Bullit always gave him to go hunting on his own. The leopard had been mortally wounded, but not killed outright. It had still enough strength left to pin Kihoro down and rake him with its claws till a chance stroke from the tracker's machete pierced the beast's heart.

When she had finished telling me this, Patricia was breathing fast, with one hand tightly clasped in the other. I asked her if she was proud of Kihoro.

"He is absolutely fearless," Patricia said.

"And your father too, I think?"

"Shut up!" she cried. "I won't have it!"

I had become accustomed to Patricia's lightning changes of mood, but was still struck, now, by the expression of intense unhappiness which abruptly suffused her face. Only a sudden attack of unbearable physical pain, one would have thought, could have turned her cheeks so ashen beneath their sunburn, or twisted her face and mouth into such an expression of agony.

"W-white people have no right to hunt," Patricia burst out, in a choking, breathless voice. "I can't stand them killing the animals. It's different for the natives. That's fair enough. They live with the beasts. They're like the beasts —and just about as well armed. But these Europeans, with their heavy-caliber rifles and pouchfuls of cartridges! And there's no *reason* for it. They just want to amuse themselves. To count their heads—"

The little girl's voice rose on a high, hysterical note. "I *hate* all white hunters," she screamed. "I hate them! I hate them!"

Her eyes were fixed on mine, and she instantly picked up my faintly interrogative glance. Her voice dropped to a scared whisper. "No," she said, "I don't include my father. There's no better man living. He does the animals nothing but good. I hate hearing about all those he once killed."

"How did you find out about it?" I asked.

"Oh, he used to talk about his exploits to Mummy and his friends, when I was still very tiny. He thought I didn't understand. Now I can't stand the thought of those days. I simply can't bear him to mention them. It's just that I love him too much."

Then there came back to me, in all its full significance, the way Patricia had looked at her father the night before, in their bungalow, willing him not to go on with his story about hunting lions among the Serenguetti.

Patricia wound down the window, put her cropped head out, and drew in a deep lungful of the hot, billowing dust thrown up by our wheels. When I saw her face again, there was no sign of the agony she had just passed through: only delighted, if impatient, anticipation. She snapped out an order to Bogo, and our car turned off onto a rough, twisting track.

It may have been due either to the bad surface or the direction in which we were now going—straight for the mysterious forest and the great beasts' hidden sanctuary —but Bogo was driving extremely badly: an unusual thing for him. The springs groaned over potholes; the brakes squealed and jerked; and Bogo crashed his gears horribly. Our advance was marked by the most frightful racket imaginable.

Patricia suddenly told him to pull up. If he didn't terrify the animals, she said, he would make them dangerously angry. Then she gripped my arm and told me to follow her. She stood on tiptoe and whispered in my ear: "*He* is quite close to us now."

She jumped out of the car and set off straight for the thorny jungle confronting us.

2

Throughout the whole of our march every movement Patricia made, as it were, was designed to protect and assist me. She pushed aside the dense scrub to let me pass through after her, looped up brambles and thorny branches out of my path, warned me of approaching difficulties and, at a pinch, hacked a way clear for me. Following in her footsteps, I skirted round the foot of a hill, avoided a swamp, climbed a steep ridge, and plunged headlong into apparently impenetrable bush. From time to time I had to make my way on hands and knees, or even crawl on my belly.

When at last Patricia stopped, we were in a ravine. Above us on either side the jungle sprang up from the cliff edge as dense and impenetrable as a wall. Patricia listened intently for a long while, watching the direction of the wind. Then, in her very quietest voice, she said: "Don't move. Don't even breathe till I tell you. Keep a sharp lookout. It's terribly important."

She moved away effortlessly to the top of the ravine, and was swallowed up among the bushes. I was alone in the stillest, heaviest silence that Equatorial Africa knows; the silence which comes when the sun has just passed its noon zenith, and the air is charged with fiery, searing heat.

I was deserted and lost in a parched, labyrinthine jungle, incapable of recognizing the right track even if I found it, my sole link with the outside world this small girl who had just disappeared into the scrub.

I was sweating already, and now I began to shiver, in quick sharp spasms that came with increasing frequency, and ran the whole length of my body. They were produced not by fear, but rather by something both outside and beyond the normal range of fear as we understand it. It was not provoked by any sense of danger. I trembled because every second now brought me closer to an encounter, perhaps even an alliance, totally remote from accepted human experience. I knew now what my instinctive presentiment had been. Supposing it turned out to be justified—

The tremors came faster and faster, and my fear grew

with every moment I waited. But there was no pleasure in the world for which I would have forgone this terrified agony of anticipation. Then a high, clear, childish laugh, charged with delight and wonder, rang out in the sultry silence like a peal of tiny bells. And the laughter which answered it was more extraordinary still—simply because it *was* a laugh. Certainly, search my brain and five senses as I will, I can't find any other word to describe that vast, good-natured growl, so vibrant with power and pure animal joy. It couldn't be true. It just *could not* be true. Now both laughs sounded together: treble bells above a rumbling descant. When they stopped, I heard Patricia calling me. Slipping and stumbling, I hauled myself up the side of the ravine, using the bushes for hand holds. Then I pushed my way through the quickset thicket at the top, my hands torn, bleeding, and full of thorns.

On the far side of this thicket I found a wide, open plain, with close-cropped grass underfoot. At its very edge stood a single tree. This tree was not particularly tall; but innumerable long, powerful branches radiated out from its gnarled and massive trunk, like spokes from a wheel, to form a kind of gigantic parasol. In the shade cast by this tree lay a lion, its head turned in my direction. It was a magnificent specimen, full-grown and at the height of its physical powers, with a glossy, resplendent coat. It lay on one flank, with its muzzle resting on the ground, and the great mane bristling out all round like a halo.

Then, between its gigantic front paws—it was playfully baring and sheathing its claws all the while—I saw Patricia. Her back rested against the great beast's front, and her neck was within easy reach of its half-open jaws.

One of her hands was scratching about in its great shaggy pelt.

My first thought was: King is the right name for him. He's a royal animal if ever there was one. Which shows how little I was protected at this moment either by my reason or my instinct.

The lion raised his head and growled: he had seen me. A strange torpor seemed to paralyze all my muscles. His tail thrashed the sluggish air, and exploded against his flank like the crack of a whip. At that instant I stopped trembling: ordinary common or garden fear now froze me. In one quick flash of illumination I saw the whole truth: Patricia was mad, and I had caught her madness. What special grace protected her still I could not tell; but it hardly extended to me.

The lion's growl swelled in his throat, and his tail thrashed still more violently. A toneless, unexpressive, neutral voice said: "Don't move—and don't be afraid. Just wait."

With one hand Patricia tugged violently at the huge, ruff-like mane; with the other, she began to scratch the lion between its eyes. While thus occupied she talked to it, in an odd sing-song voice: "Quiet now, King. You're going to be quiet. This is a new friend, King. Listen, King—this is a friend—a friend—a friend—"

At first she spoke in English; then she switched to various native dialects. But the name "King" recurred ceaselessly. After a little the angry lashing of the tail stopped, and the growling slowly died away into silence. The lion's great head sank back on the grass, and its mane (which for an instant had risen) now once more half-covered it.

"Take one step forward," the toneless voice said.

I did so; the lion made no move. But now his eyes remained fixed on me.

"Now another step," Patricia said, still in the same flat voice.

I advanced gingerly. Step by step, with each successive command, I saw the distance between the lion and myself diminish, in the most terrifying way. The creature seemed to be smelling and savoring my flesh—judging its bulk, relishing its taste and the blood it contained.

I had recourse to every possible argument that might help me to outface those unwinking yellow eyes, which never left mine. I told myself that even the most savage dogs love children and obey their commands. I remembered a gypsy animal-tamer I had known once, who, every evening, put his head inside the jaws of an enormous lion. His brother acted as keeper for the circus animals, and when they were on the road in cold weather, this chap would doss down between a couple of his tigers for the sake of the warmth. And, in the last resort, I knew that Kihoro was near enough to help me in an emergency.

But it was in vain that I filled my head with such reassuring notions. As that toneless whisper drew me forward, step by step, toward the great reclining beast, they lost all value or meaning. I could not disobey the voice. It was, I knew beyond any doubt, my only chance of remaining alive, the one force—however hazardous and uncertain—that held the lion, Patricia, and myself in a spellbound, uneasy balance.

Yet how long could it last? I took one more step. If I stretched out my hand now, I would actually touch the lion's body. This time he did not growl, but his throat and jaws yawned open like a gleaming steel trap, and he half-rose to his feet.

"King!" Patricia cried out. "Down, King!"

I hardly recognized her voice, so self-confident and assured was it, so dominating, so certain of its own power. In the same instant, Patricia hit the great beast between the eyes, as hard as she could. The lion turned his head, blinked, and lay down peacefully again.

"Quick—put your hand here," Patricia said.

I did as she told me. Now my hand rested on King's neck, just behind his mane.

"Keep quite still," Patricia said, and stroked King silently for a little, her hand going up and down between his eyes, where she had hit him. Then she told me to rub his neck. I did so.

"Faster," Patricia told me. "Harder."

The lion turned his head toward me, sniffed my scent carefully, yawned, and shut his eyes. Patricia let her hand drop from his muzzle. I went on briskly stroking the coarse, tawny coat. King lay quite still.

"That's all right," Patricia said, quite seriously. "You're friends now." Then she began to laugh; and the innocent mischievousness which I so adored in her turned this laughter to pure childish glee.

"You got an awful fright, didn't you?" she asked me.

"I'm still frightened," I said.

At the sound of my voice, the huge lion opened one yellow eye and fixed it on me.

"Don't stop stroking his neck," Patricia said. "And go on talking—quickly."

"I'm still frightened," I repeated. "Still frightened. Still frightened—"

The lion listened for a moment, yawned, stretched (I felt the huge knotted muscles swell under my hand), folded his paws and lay still.

"Good," Patricia said. "Now he knows you—your scent, the feel of your skin, your voice, everything. We can sit down and talk now."

My stroking became slower, and finally stopped. I took my hand away from King's neck.

"Come and sit here," Patricia said, pointing to a patch of dry grass beside one of King's paws, and only one step away from it. I bent my knees inch by inch till I was in a squatting position, and then lowered myself to the ground as carefully as I could.

The lion's head turned in my direction. His eyes went over me, examining my hands and shoulders and face. This inspection was twice repeated. I watched in stupefied amazement, my fear steadily diminishing. In King's eyes I could discern comprehensible, *human* expressions, to which I found no difficulty in attaching the appropriate label—curiosity, good-natured amiability, that generous kindliness which the strong display to those weaker than themselves.

"Everything's going well—everything's going wonderfully," Patricia chanted to herself. She was no longer addressing King; her words were an expression of the emotional unity which bound her to this free, natural world, where all bars and enclosures were unknown. And by Patricia's intercession, through her as intermediary, this world was now mine also. I was discovering, with a delight untouched by any regard for my personal safety, that age-old fears and immemorial ignorance were vanishing from my mind as though by exorcism. I saw, too, that the friendly relationship now establishing itself between man and lion proved fallacious the old notion of separate, mutually exclusive kingdoms for mankind and the brutes. Here we stood side by side on a single—yet infinitely varied—ladder of creation.

Hypnotized, only half-conscious of what I was doing, I bent down toward that royal head and copied Patricia's gesture of affection: with the tips of my fingers I gently stroked the dark-brown triangular patch between King's great golden eyes. A slight tremor ran through his mane; his heavy jowl stirred, and he half-opened his jaws. There was an amiable gleam from those terrible white fangs.

"Look," Patricia said. "Look carefully. He's smiling at you!"

How could I doubt the truth of what she said? Had I not already heard King's laughter, from the ravine?

"I picked the best time to introduce you to him," Patricia went on. "He's had a good kill, and he's glutted—" Here she tapped the lion's muscular belly. "It's the hottest part of the day, and there's plenty of shade here. He's feeling very pleased with life."

Patricia slid between King's paws, and rubbed her cropped hair against his shaggy breast.

"There you are," she said. "There's nothing very difficult or frightening about it, is there?"

"Only because you're here with me."

Hardly had I uttered these words when a radical change took place in my mood, and my attitude to my present surroundings. Up to this moment the extremities of terror and delight I had experienced had kept me in a tranced state where miracles seemed no more than natural. Now I reverted abruptly to normal, and saw the fantastic quality of the situation in terms more appropriate to my ordinary condition. I looked at the remote savannah; at this tree, struggling in its barren soil, with thorns instead of leaves crowning it; at the King of Beasts, the most terrible carnivore alive, sprawling beneath its branchy shade, lord of his own domain—and at myself, now stroking his forehead. I looked; and everything appeared in a new light, a profoundly modified perspective. It was all real enough, indeed, verifiable by my senses and reasoning faculties—but only because of Patricia. I was here thanks to a little girl in gray overalls who now sat curled up against a lion's shaggy breast for all the world like a silkworm.

How could I put into words the unique feeling of tenderness she inspired in me, or express the unparalleled debt of gratitude I owed her? In the end I was compelled to fall back on an ordinary, banal gesture. I said: "Can I kiss you, Patricia?"

Perhaps the intensity of my feelings had found its way into my voice; perhaps, too, Patricia was unused to this kind of effusive approach. At all events her cheeks now took on that exquisite color, midway between rose-pink and a tanned brown, which she always displayed when flushed with pleasure. She quickly disengaged her hand from the gigantic paw that covered it, and offered me her face to kiss. It smelled of lavender soap, and lion, and the scent of the bush.

King's great yellow eyes followed all our movements with unflagging attention. When he saw my head approach Patricia's, and my lips brush her cheek, the big lion repeated the motion which Patricia had described as a smile; and when she slipped back to her place between his paws, he gently licked her hair.

Patricia laughed and said: "He often kisses me himself."

So the three of us sat there, united in the common friendship of warm earth and midday shade.

"Tell me, Patricia," I asked, "how did it all begin?"

The girl suddenly gripped the lion's mane with both fists, and drew the great shaggy head toward her in a violent, almost convulsive gesture: she seemed to be looking at her own reflection in those golden eyes.

She said: "You can have no idea what a tiny, helpless creature he was when Kihoro gave him to me as a present."

She gazed at King again, and her childish features betrayed the same feelings of incredulity, tenderness, and sad resignation a mother shows when she looks at her grown-up son, and remembers the newborn baby he once was.

"At the time," Patricia went on, with a little sigh, "Kihoro had already lost the sight of one eye, but that rhino hadn't yet squashed him against the tree. Besides, I was much smaller then: Kihoro wasn't my own private servant in those days. When my father went on tours of inspection in those parts of the Park which no one else ever explores, Kihoro used to go with him. Kihoro's got an even better nose for a trail than my father, you know. Well, one morning, Kihoro found a tiny lion cub in the jungle, in a hollow tree. He was only two days old at the outside, Kihoro said. His eyes weren't open yet, and he was crying like a baby. He was all alone."

Patricia rubbed one cheek against King's mane.

"But how did he come to be abandoned?" I asked.

The child curled up one finger and said: "Probably his parents went hunting, and followed their prey outside the Reserve. Then, when they reached an area where my father could not protect them any more, they must have been shot by white hunters."

She curled up another finger. "There's another possibility. The mother might have had a large litter, and was too exhausted to go on looking after the weakest cub." Then she pressed her cheek closer to the majestic mane and concluded: "Or, quite simply, she didn't love him enough." Her voice was charged with compassion: it was as though the great lion still lay helpless and without any protection against all the dangers and cruelties of the bush.

"You've never seen anything so minute," Patricia said, rocking to and fro between those monumental paws. "Honestly, when we found him King was no bigger than my father's two fists put together. He was terribly skinny, without a single hair on his body, and whimpering with hunger and thirst and terror. Mummy said he was just like a real newborn baby. She said he was too sickly to live. But I was determined he wasn't going to die."

Then Patricia told me, in great detail and with a kind of yearning nostalgia, just how she had nursed the lion cub back to life and strength, and cared for it. At first she kept it going with a feeding-bottle; after a while she began to give it sugar, and then she got it used to porridge. It slept in her bed, snuggled up beside her. She made sure it never caught cold. She rubbed it down when it got into a sweat, and on chilly evenings wrapped it up in her own woolen jumpers. When it had filled out and was really sleek, Patricia gave a christening-party for it.

"I found his name," she said. "Nobody believed me at the time, but I knew one day he would be a real king among beasts."

Once again Patricia gave that curious, maternal sigh of regret; but it was in a characteristically childish tone that she went on: "You can't imagine how fast a lion grows. By the time I really understood how to look after him he was as big as I was."

Then her face altered abruptly: she looked not a day more than her real age as she said: "Then, *then* we began to play. And King used to do whatever I told him."

Patricia roughly pushed aside the huge paw that could have flattened her into pulp at a single stroke, and got up. She stood there, tense, jaws clenched, and unimaginably fragile when compared with the huge dozing beast lying in front of her. Excitement and pride, the over-riding demands of possessiveness, now showed clearly in her face. It was not hard to guess what she had in mind. She wanted to convince me—and herself through me—that King in his splendid prime, at the very height of his physical powers, still remained *hers,* as absolutely dependent on her care as the abandoned cub who had only gone on living because she willed it.

"He still does what I tell him," she cried. *"Always.* Now watch: I'll show you."

I hardly thought it possible that I could experience yet another kind of terror in this one day: yet Patricia evoked it in me, though not so much on my own account as hers. She suddenly bent her knees, sprang as high in the air as she could, and came down, both feet together, on the lion's flank, with a pile-driving energy that doubled the speed of her descent. She bounced off onto the ground and repeated her experiment, several times. Next, she hammered away at King's belly with her doubled-up fists, and butted him with her head. Finally she flung herself on his mane, seized it in both hands, and began to shake his terrible head in all directions. All the time she was shouting: "Come on, King! *Do* something, can't you? You don't scare me, you great hulking lump! Stand up, King! We'll see who's the master here!"

The great lion rolled over on his back, stretched out one paw and opened his great dark jaws.

Kihoro, Kihoro, for God's sake shoot, I prayed silently. She's going to be mauled—

But the angry roar I had been expecting did not come. Instead the air hummed with that vast, hoarse, delighted purr, that happy growling sound which was King's way of laughing. The huge paw, far from descending on Patricia and tearing her to shreds, approached her very gently, claws sheathed, picked her up, and deposited her with great delicacy on the ground. Patricia returned to the attack, and King repeated his previous move. But he was beginning to enjoy the game. Not content now simply with scooping Patricia up and putting her down, he batted her away as though she were a ball. Each stroke was a miracle of timing, accuracy, and resilience. He used the flat of his paw like a velvety tennis racket, hitting the child with exactly the force needed to make her fly through the air, yet not hard enough to inflict the slightest injury.

Patricia struggled, without success, to dodge this soft, flailing attack. Then she flung herself on King's ears, pulled them savagely, and stuck her thumbs in his eyes. King laughed harder than ever. He shook his head and rolled over on Patricia, yet in such a way that there was never any danger of her being crushed by his weight. Then the girl popped up on his other flank, and the whole gambit began again.

When Patricia finally gave up her game she was tousle-haired, breathless, and covered with sweat. Her gray overalls were smothered in tawny hairs, stuck all over with thorns and wisps of dry grass. Panting gently, she stretched herself out close to the lion. He licked her hand and the back of her neck. Patricia gave an exhausted grin. King had given a fine display both of his intelligence and his obedience to her.

"I was terribly afraid for you," I said, in a low voice.

"For *me?*"

She sat up, leaning on one elbow, and stared at me, frowning and tight-lipped, as though I had just insulted her.

"Do you imagine this lion would ever dream of hurting me?" she demanded. "Do you think I haven't got absolute control over his actions?"

A queer light flickered in her eyes.

"Well, you're wrong," she continued. "If I give the word, King will tear you to pieces on the spot. Shall we try it?"

Before I could reply, Patricia pushed the lion's head round in my direction, pointed at me with one finger, and emitted a strange sound from her throat: a short, deep, muffled call, with whistling overtones. King was on his feet with one quick surge of those huge muscles. It was the first time I had seen him standing erect, and he seemed enormous. His mane flared out stiffly, and his tail lashed from flank to flank with fierce violence. The color of his eyes had changed from soft gold to a glacial yellow. His shoulders bunched for the spring. He was going to—

"No, King. *No. Down,*" Patricia said. She placed one hand on King's nostrils: they were dilated with anger. She gently clicked her tongue several times, and King's fury ebbed away. I must have been very pale, because Patricia, after examining my face, began to laugh with malicious glee. Yet she remained as affectionate as before.

"That'll teach you not to be scared for me," she said, one hand going to and fro on the great lion's neck. King's muscles were still tense and quivering.

"You'd better go now," she went on, cheerfully. "King will be suspicious of you for the rest of the day. But he'll have forgotten all about it by next time."

She explained how I should get back. All I had to do was get to the ridge, which was clearly visible from the far side of the ravine. After that it was just a matter of keeping straight on toward the sun.

Having given me my instructions, Patricia jumped up onto King's back. I no longer existed for either of them.

3

It was getting late in the afternoon, and the animals were beginning to emerge from their lairs. Yet I barely noticed them; between the external world and my awareness of it stood King, Patricia's friend King, the great lion of Kilimanjaro. Behind every bush, in each fold of open country,

I seemed to see his mane and his golden eyes, the yawning cavern of his open jaws, the vast paws that played with a little girl as though she were a ball. When I got back to the car, and Bogo began talking about herds on the move and migrating tribesmen, the same obsession ensured that I scarcely listened to a word he said. In fact, I didn't realize what he was driving at till the column of marching Masai debouched on the main road. They, at last, brought me back to my actual surroundings.

I had often before in the course of my life met with trekking nomads, in many different countries. But even the poorest and most vagrant had always possessed some sort of baggage, threadbare and primitive though it might be, which was carried by pack animals—at the very worst by a few starving donkeys. These Masai, on the other hand, traveled without so much as a single bag or package, without even a tent to shelter them at night or a cooking-pot in which to prepare their food. They carried no burdens or impedimenta of any kind whatsoever.

The convoy moved in hollow square, with the herd at its center. The latter was composed of about a hundred lean, scraggy cows, whose ribs and backbones stood out with skeletal clarity. Their slack, lackluster skin was covered with cuts and scratches: swarms of flies gorged themselves on the oozing blood. But the tribe—or, to be more precise, the tribal clan whose sole possessions these wretched cattle were—showed none of the usual signs of extreme poverty. They were neither terrified, nor stupid, nor miserable, nor servile. The women in their tattered cotton wraps, the men with that fold of cloth slung over the shoulder on which they carried their spears—all alike marched along with a firm, swinging step, holding themselves erect, their bearing proud and independent. Loud shouts and bursts of laughter rippled up and down the column. No one in the world was richer than these folk, who owned nothing and had no desire to do so.

This file of Masai took up the entire width of the road. It would have been perfectly easy for them to close up their ranks and let our car pass; but the idea never even occurred to them. Bogo had to drive off the road himself, and go bumping through the undergrowth, before we finally overtook them. At the head of the column marched the young warriors of the clan, three *moranes* with their strange topknots of dressed hair and red clay. The first of the three—who was also the tallest, the handsomest, and the most insolent—was Oriunga.

I leaned out the window and called out *"Kouahéri!"* the Masai greeting, to him. The children and some of the women who marched along behind the *morane* returned this formal salutation very cheerfully; but Oriunga himself did not so much as turn his head.

I remained in my bungalow, alone, till nightfall. I completely unpacked all my luggage, and set the contents in some sort of order. I put my books on the bookshelves, and my provisions in the kitchen. I no longer knew how long my stay in the National Park was liable to last. It entirely depended on King. Could I afford to haggle over a few more days if they might prove like the one I had just spent?

When it was time to go over to the Bullits' bungalow for dinner, I felt a little apprehensive. I was afraid that I might find a similar atmosphere to that of the previous night: elaborate pretense, forced gaiety, with a screaming nervous tension underlying them. But the minute I got inside I realized that my fear had been quite unjustified.

Sybil, it was true, had put on evening dress; Bullit had plastered down his red hair with water; Patricia was wearing her sky-blue dress and patent-leather shoes, and the dining-room was lit by candles. But all these things, which twenty-four hours ago had produced an unhappy, artificial atmosphere, tonight (through what agency I could not tell) gave the party an intimate, sophisticated charm.

Sybil was careful not to make any reference to her uncontrollable outburst of the previous evening. To judge by appearances, it would seem that this crisis had been completely forgotten by her. It also appeared that, so far as Sybil was concerned, the conventional rules of social etiquette were only necessary for a first visit, and that thereafter people could revert to their normal behavior and conversational tone. Thus I at once got the impression that she was treating me as a friend.

Bullit thanked me with unaffected delight for bringing him a bottle of whisky.

"I was just running out, old boy," he murmured in my ear. "Between you and me, I sometimes think I punish the stuff a bit too hard."

As for this polite, demure Patricia, she had nothing at all in common with the wild-haired maenad whom I had seen stand beneath a spreading, shady tree and work her will on the great lion of Kilimanjaro.

I forbade myself to think about King. I was afraid that, in my hypnotized obsession with him, I might suddenly speak his name aloud. I had only too clear a recollection of the affect he had produced on Sybil.

But we had hardly sat down to dinner when she brought

the subject up herself. Smiling, she said: "I hear that Patricia showed you round our Reserve today—and introduced you to her best friend."

This change of front was so complete that, in my astonishment, I decided she couldn't be referring to the lion at all.

"Ah, yes," I said. "You mean—?" And I carefully let the question trail away uncompleted.

"Why, King of course!" said Sybil, cheerfully. "I hope you found him a beautiful, intelligent, and altogether magnificent beast," she added; and I saw that, in a very light and affectionate way, she was pulling Patricia's leg.

I said: "I have never seen anything more astonishing in my life than the power your daughter has over this wild creature."

Sybil's eyes remained as tranquil as before. "Patricia came home early today. We had time to go on with this morning's lessons."

"I promise you, Mummy," Patricia said, "I *promise* you I'll be as clever as you one day. *And* I'll dress as well as your friend Lise."

Sybil shook her head gently. "It won't be as simple as that, darling," she said.

Patricia half-closed her eyes: it was impossible to make out their expression behind the long, drooping lashes.

"I haven't seen those school photographs of you and Lise for a long time now," she said. "Would you care to show them to us after dinner?"

"There's a good girl, Pat," Bullit said. "Look how pleased Mummy is."

Sybil's normally pale and faded cheeks were, indeed, faintly tinged with color. "I'd love to show you those old pictures," she told me. "I only hope you won't be too bored by them. Still, you'll have something to make up for it. John's got a whole collection of snaps of King, when he was a cub."

Sybil and her daughter said nothing to one another at this moment; they did not even exchange glances. Were they even aware that all day long they had pursued a secret, subtle, diplomatic agreement—and had, finally, negotiated an instinctive truce, a happy compromise for them both?

When the meal was over, both Bullit and his wife went out in search of their photographic souvenirs. Sybil came back first, carrying a large flat album, gilt-edged and bound in the most ghastly cloth boards imaginable.

"I didn't choose it," she said. "It was a good-conduct prize awarded by our old headmistress."

There was a wistful half-smile on her lips. She knew very well that her album was in the most appalling taste; but this very awfulness had its own value for her, since it recalled a period which she cherished dearly.

Though I tried as hard as I could, I failed to summon up more than the barest expressions of polite appreciation as I went through these insipid photographs. The most they ever achieved was a kind of disarming silliness. But Patricia showed a most lively interest in them. Was this the result of deliberate pretense or simple affection? Or was it even possible that this distant world really stimulated her imagination and sensibilities? After all, the girls who moved in it were more or less of her own age.

Whether it was in fact genuine or assumed, Patricia's sincerity *seemed* beyond all question. She gave little squeals of delight or admiration. She listened eagerly, and again and again encouraged Sybil to enlarge on some snapshot or other. She continually praised the appearance, clothes, coiffure, and hair ribbons of one particular schoolgirl who, to me, looked no different from any of the others—but was, in fact, Lise Darbois.

This discussion was cut short by the return of Bullit, carrying a big strong envelope stuffed full of photographs. He put it down on a long, narrow side table and said: "Sorry to have been so long, but I honestly couldn't remember where I'd stacked this lot away. They're pretty old, you know."

He slid out the first bundle of snaps and spread them side by side along the table.

"First part of our serial, ladies and gentlemen," he announced. "King in the nursery."

"Don't make a joke of it, John," Sybil said, in a low voice. She stood bent over the photographs, examining them. Aloud she went on: "They haven't been taken out of their drawer for ages. I'd forgotten what an enchanting little creature he used to be. Look at these!"

She held out about a dozen snaps to me. Each showed the most sweet little animal imaginable, as she had said, and rather clumsy, too, with its squarish head and scarce-opened eyes. In all of them he was with a child who looked as though she might be Patricia's younger sister—sometimes curled up in her arms, sometimes clinging to her shoulder, and sometimes sucking away at the feeding-bottle she held out to him.

"Is that *really* King?" I exclaimed, despite myself.

Bullit ran one hand through his hair. It had had time to dry, and was now suddenly and noticeably ruffled, in every sense of the word. Embarrassed by an access of sentimentality, which made his hoarse voice huskier still, he said: "Even I find it hard to believe that that pint-sized little creature could—"

Sybil broke in softly: "I've never in my life seen anything so defenseless and gentle and full of natural affection."

Only Patricia said nothing; nor would she look at the photographs.

"I would have adored to look after him in those days," Sybil went on, "but Patricia would never let me. If I so much as tried to lay a finger on that lion cub, she used to fly into the most frightful rages."

Just for an instant Patricia's face lost its placidity, and became suffused with the violent feeling I had observed during her circus act with King, under that shady tree out in the bush.

She said: "King belonged to me."

Hastily I held out a photograph to her and asked her to explain what was going on in it. All I could see was a shapeless wooly ball, from which emerged two neat little ears and about half of a small round muzzle. Both eyes were tight shut.

"He'd caught cold," Patricia said, "so I wrapped him up in my sweater."

She sounded as though she might unbend a little; but just as I was on the point of asking her another question she said, curtly: "I'm afraid I was very small in those days. I've forgotten all about it."

This was a lie; and I knew it. I knew it from what Patricia herself had told me as she sat happily between King's paws that afternoon. She remembered every least detail of the lion cub's development. But she had no wish to recall those lost days when King depended entirely on her—

not now, when at this very moment the great beast was prowling freely through the African night, far beyond her reach.

"If you want to find out more," she said, "you'd better ask my father. He took the photographs. He'll tell you anything you want to know."

Then she turned back to the other album, with its awful lemon-colored binding, and Sybil went with her. The two of them settled down in the same armchair and began to talk in whispers. I could now give my undivided attention —and there was nothing I wanted to do more—to the series of snaps which Bullit laid out, one after another, for my entertainment.

He had sorted them into chronological order—with such meticulous accuracy, indeed, that I followed every step in King's growth as though on slow-motion film. I felt I was spying on some secret process of animal life as I watched King's extraordinary metamorphosis from a tiny cub, nursed by a child, into that splendid great creature, glorious in his strength and majesty, whose golden eyes still seemed to stare at me from under their royal mane. First he was a kitten, then a cat, then a recognizable cub, then a half-grown beast. Next he appeared as an unmistakable lion, but with his full size and power yet to come. Finally, there was King, just as I had seen him a few hours earlier.

I turned the snaps over and examined the dates inscribed on each one, in Bullit's heavy square script. I said: "And that transformation took less than a year from start to finish!"

Bullit nodded. "More's the pity," he said. "These cubs grow much faster and bigger than we do. But that doesn't change the way they feel about people. Look at this next lot."

The film continued to unwind, and what it showed us was, progressively, a greater and greater strain on my credulity. Here was this gigantic lion sitting beside Bullit in his Land Rover, or at table between him and Patricia. Here he was again, furiously tearing apart the *kiboko* with which he had just been punished—but not so much as growling at his master. Here he was playing with the rangers, and here licking Sybil's hand. Like an automaton I repeated the word "Incredible!" as each new shot appeared.

"What's so incredible about it?" Bullit remarked at length, in a mildly irritated voice. "When I was a kid we found a lion cub abandoned in the bush—just like King. We took him home and kept him on the farm. For five whole years he stayed with us, and never harmed a living soul, white or black. Never killed an animal, either. When my father was transferred to a desk job in town we had to turn that lion loose in the bush. Believe it or not, we had to teach him how to hunt and kill first."

"What about this, then?" I asked. The photograph I had in my hand showed King in a forest clearing, together with other lions.

"Oh, that was taken when I was traveling round the Reserve," Bullit said. "I just happened to run across him. He was having a high old time with a few of his chums. That used to happen quite often—"

"But he always came back," Patricia said harshly. She was still in the big armchair with her mother.

Bullit gathered up the photographs carelessly and stuffed them back into their envelope.

"Perhaps we ought to join the ladies again," he said.

Sybil asked me endless questions about Paris and London. What were the latest books and plays? How had fashions changed? Who was giving the really big parties now? From time to time she would sigh nostalgically. Then Patricia would snuggle up closer to her, and Sybil would caress her daughter's straight, cropped hair. Every time she made this gesture it was duplicated by a vague, blurred shadow on the curtains.

Bullit sat watching his wife and child, a black West Indian cigar stuck in one corner of his mouth. He seemed happy and relaxed: it must have been a very good cigar.

4

When I got back to my bungalow, the electric generator had already been turned off. But one of the native boys had lit a hurricane lamp for me and put it on the veranda table. I sat down and began to reflect on the events of the day.

My nerves were on edge: the peaceful evening I had just spent had, oddly enough, strained them far more than the near-hysterical outbursts and scenes of the previous night. This all-pervasive atmosphere of mellow amiability and relaxed good will was not, I told myself, a true guide to what the Bullits were feeling or thinking. These waters were deceptively still; their stagnation contained danger and disease.

How was Sybil's cheerful acceptance of King to be reconciled with the loathing she had shown for him the day before? What common factor was there between Patricia's enthusiasm for her mother's photograph album and her wild sport with the great tawny beast? Once again the lion insinuated himself into my mind. Was it imagination, or could I hear him growling to himself, far away in the darkness of the bush? It might have been only the faint and distant thunder of a tropical summer storm—or my own steadily mounting obsession.

As I said, my nerves were very much on edge. Accordingly, when Bullit suddenly materialized beside me, I could appreciate and share Sybil's hatred for cat-footed people. I nearly cried out in fright as his huge shadow fell across the circle of lamplight.

Bullit had changed back into his bush shirt, khaki slacks, and heavy boots. His hair was once more a shaggy tangled mass. In one hand he carried the bottle of whisky I had given him. It was still half full.

"I know you've got a whole case of the stuff," he said, cutting short my protestations. "But I insist on our finishing this bottle together. Tonight. No point in keeping it—too much gone already."

Friendship radiated from his heavy features.

"It's a very long time indeed since we've enjoyed such a happy evening at home," he went on. "Your presence has a calming effect on Sybil. And the child adores you."

I hurried off in search of some glasses. Whenever I was alone with Bullit I found myself wanting a drink badly.

We sat and sipped our whisky in silence. I sensed that my companion was finding this moment of relaxation as beneficial as I did. Yet now, again, I thought I heard a distant roar echo across the stillness of the night. Bullit didn't move a muscle; I must have been mistaken. Perhaps in his case familiarity had bred indifference.

"Why didn't King stay with you indefinitely?" I asked.

"Because of Sybil. She wasn't born and brought up in East Africa. She got to a point where she couldn't bear to see his mane and claws around the place the whole time. And the way he had of leaping clear across the room at a single bound to lick her hand or jump up with his forepaws on my shoulders— He was a big brute, you know. And every time Patricia romped in the grass with him, Sybil nearly passed out with sheer fright. She began to feel a creeping horror for King. And of course, King knew it. He stopped coming up to caress her, and wouldn't let her stroke him. At that point she became so terrified that she swore she'd leave me and go back to Nairobi if I didn't get rid of King. Well, I wouldn't have minded losing King, but there was Pat to consider."

Bullit broke off at this point, and I saw by his expression that he was finding it very hard to go on. But I had become caught up in this story like a wild creature in a snare, and at all costs I had to know how it ended. Bullit, I knew instinctively, would refuse me nothing tonight.

"Well," I demanded insistently, "what happened then?"

"We both did what we had to do, Sybil and I," Bullit said. "That same morning I took King by Land Rover to the farthest boundary of the Reserve and abandoned him there; and Sybil drove Pat into Nairobi and left *her* in the best girls' school in town."

Bullit sighed deeply.

"I suppose you know we had to let Pat come home again very soon after that?"

"Yes, I had heard."

"Well," Bullit said, tapping his glass lightly on the table top for emphasis, "the day after she was back, King turned up outside the bungalow, and they were off playing games together in the clearing."

Bullit was silent for some time. Then he went on: "Sybil begged me to shoot the lion. You've got to understand how she felt. But how could I do it? Even today Pat has scarcely forgiven me for the beasts I slaughtered long before she was born."

Bullit looked up at me heavily and said: "If I had had *King's* blood on my hands—can you imagine what she would have thought?" The former great white hunter shut his eyes and shivered.

"In that case—" I persisted.

Bullit shrugged his shoulders. "We reached a compromise solution," he said. "Pat and I found the tree you visited this morning with her. Next day, when King came back to the bungalow, we all three went off there. Pat explained to King that this was where their meetings would take place in future. She really made him understand, *think*, like a— Well, you see what I'm getting at. She can do anything with him. You know that now yourself, don't you?"

"Indeed I do," I said.

"The lion was fond of me as well," Bullit said. "When I was on my way home from a tour of inspection, he'd get wind of my car from miles away, and come running to meet me. It still happens today, sometimes. I suddenly see him charging toward me in some Godforsaken part of the bush, just to give me a warm welcome. But his relationship with the child is something different again. He knew her scent and touch from the moment he was conscious of anything at all. He belongs to her forever."

Bullit poured the last of the whisky into his glass, drained it, and got up.

"One thing more," I said. "Has King got a mate and cubs of his own?"

Bullit's eyes were covered with a fine network of red veins. He said, as though he had not heard my question: "I drink too much, you know. Good night, and sleep well."

He walked heavily yet noiselessly down the veranda steps.

I did not linger on the veranda, but went straight to my room. As I opened the door I saw the little monkey, Nicholas, sitting beside my pillow. And stretched out on my bed, in pink cotton pajamas, was Patricia.

My astonishment set her off into one of her really childish bursts of laughter. She jumped off the bed, the top of her flimsy pajama jacket half open. Beneath the sunburned neck her skin was pathetically delicate and pale.

She said: "I got out by the window and climbed in here the same way. I had to. I've given my parents quite enough worry today already."

I found myself wondering whether Kihoro kept an eye on Patricia at night as well as during the daytime.

"That's why I'm only going to stay a minute," she went on. "I just came to tell you to get up very early tomorrow morning. We'll go and see the Masai organize their *manyatta*—their camp, that is. It's very curious. You wait and see."

The Masai. The flamboyant, exotic headdress of Oriunga, the *morane*, seemed to flicker before my eyes.

"All right then? At dawn tomorrow?" Patricia asked.

"At dawn tomorrow," I said.

Small monkey and small girl vanished through the window simultaneously.

5

It was in the barest part of the Reserve that Oriunga and the ancient Ol'Kalu had sought out a camping-site for their clan. The Masai are children of the great dry plains; they distrust heavily overgrown terrain. Tree cults, or the Spirit of the Forests, are alien to their instinctive temperament. The spot finally chosen by Oriunga and Ol'Kalu, therefore, was near a water hole, and on a slight rise overlooking a wide expanse of bare, parched savannah.

There was no track leading to the camp, but the ground was clear enough for a car to approach it without trouble. The going was so easy, indeed, that by sunrise we were already in sight of the bare hillside, all dotted with black figures.

"There they are!" Patricia exclaimed, leaning out of the window. "And we're here in time."

She slid back onto the seat beside me.

"Look at our two blacks," she said, laughing. "They don't feel at all happy. Do you know why?"

"Well, Bogo's scared."

"Of course he's scared," said Patricia contemptuously. "He's a town-bred Kikuyu."

"What about Kihoro?"

"Oh, he's not *scared* by the Masai—he just hates them. He'd like to kill them all."

Her voice took on the faintly superior tone that always crept into it when she was enlightening my ignorance.

"Kihoro belongs to the Wakamba," she told me, "and the Wakamba are very brave people. Besides, they've always been fighting the Masai. Even today, despite all the Government's laws against such things, they still have occasional pitched battles—to the death. They occupy adjacent territory, you see."

Patricia leaned forward to the front seat where the old one-eyed tracker sat, and whispered a few words to him in his native dialect. Kihoro bared his withered gums in a ferocious grin, and patted his rifle.

"You're deliberately rousing him," I told the child. "Why?"

"To make him really dangerously angry," she said. "When he goes too far, I calm him down and get him under control again. It's a game I play."

I said: "But he doesn't know it's a game."

"Of course he doesn't. There wouldn't be any fun in it if he did."

Kihoro the one-eyed, I thought; the great lion King. What strange new partners would the future allot Patricia for her private game? And in what unexplored territories would she play it?

By now we had reached the bottom of the little hills. Patricia jumped out of the car before it even stopped. The tropical sun was rising in all its glory; but the pure dawn air was heavy with a manurish stink that put me in mind of a badly neglected stable.

"Come on, quick!" Patricia called out to me. "They're beginning."

She dragged me along the low ridge before us till we reached the summit of the hill. Here there was a flat open space, in the shape of a large oval. Round the outer edge of this space ran a double zareba of thorn bushes, intersected by trenches. Inside the enclosure lay a thick, sticky, yellowish mess of half-liquid cow dung. Its odor was unbelievably disgusting.

A crowd of natives—men, women, and children alike—were busy with this filthy stuff—pounding, kneading, trampling it to give it some sort of consistency of texture. Patricia addressed them in their own tongue. At first these fierce faces showed nothing but surprise at being thus addressed by a small white girl. Then even the most stony and cruel of them insensibly softened. The women uttered shrill yelps of laughter, and the children shrieked with delight.

I looked round for Oriunga, but failed to see any of the three *moranes*. I spotted old Ol'Kalu, however, and greeted him. He recognized me at once. "*Kouahéri*," he called out, and then signaled to his people to go on with their work.

The fetid stench became thicker and more powerful than ever. I recoiled instinctively, holding my breath. Patricia, however, seemed not in the least put out. This was the little girl who had left a delicate whiff of soap and lavender water behind her when she left my bungalow the night before: indeed, I could still smell it on her. This was the child whose sense of smell was so acute that she could pick out each individual scent, of plant or beast, in the bush. Yet now she was snuffing up this repugnant stink, her eyes shining with pleasure. She was like those upper-class children who are born and bred in the Big House, but grow up around the farmyard with a crowd of village urchins, and get far more enjoyment out of filthy jobs like cleaning out cowsheds and stables than from occupations more suited to their station in life.

"You know, they're sly, these Masai," Patricia said. She clearly wanted me to partake of her excited enthusiasm. "Really intelligent, too. Fancy making houses out of cowpats! They never live anywhere for long, you see, and they haven't got shovels or tools of any kind. So they've invented this idea for themselves. They pen up their herd for a whole day and night on the spot where they want their camp. Then they knead the dung and get it ready for building."

"And after that?" I asked.

"You'll see," Patricia said. "Hold on: they're beginning now."

Round the sticky mass several men were now erecting hurdles. On top of these they fixed an arching roof of branches, which acquired some cohesion from the thorns and spines that covered them. The hurdles were arranged in an oval pattern that matched the shape of the little hilltop plateau. In a very short space of time they had built a kind of large open-work hut that ran the whole length of the open ground. It was very low, not standing higher than the chests of its builders, and bristling with thorns.

"Now then," Patricia cried, "watch what happens next!"

Old Ol'Kalu gave an order; and at once all of them, men, women, and children alike, set to work digging up the soft, steaming muck they had just been preparing, and began to spread it over the framework of branches. Some of them used their hands, others the goatskin bottles that normally held milk or drinking-water. The stinking, half-liquid, brownish paste was slapped on the hurdles, where it ran down dripping to the ground, and finally solidified into a wall. By the same process the arching thorn branches were turned into a roof. As quickly as possible this first layer was reinforced by a second, as the community showered their new home with fresh daubs of cow dung.

"In a few hours the sun will dry it all out as hard as a bone," Patricia said. "Wonderful, isn't it?"

Although it was still early in the morning, thick, droning swarms of horseflies had already settled on the wet muck.

"Let's go now," I called out to Patricia. "There's nothing more to see, is there?"

Two little Masai girls were cracking jokes at her, and exploding in gales of giggles.

"Just a minute," Patricia said. "I'm having such fun—!" Then she ran back to me, shouting: "Do listen, it's a smashing joke, these girls thought we were married!"

"Who?"

"You and me, of course," Patricia said. She paused to savor my astonishment. Then she explained: "These kids aren't any older than me, and plenty of them are married already. That's the custom among the Masai. The rest wait till the young men of the clan have finished their time as *moranes*."

"Where are the *moranes*, by the way?"

"Over here," Patricia said. She led me across to the opposite side of the plateau from that by which we had come. At the foot of the slope—and nicely camouflaged by it—

◇◇

I saw the Masai herd, penned in a square corral constructed from thorn bushes. Among the cattle I could see the rays of the rising sun flash back from three spears and three coppery heads of dressed hair.

"We'll go down," Patricia said.

The *moranes* had just got the cattle jammed up against a big movable hurdle made of prickly branches, which formed the entrance to the corral. Patricia stood watching the young men, motionless. For their part they did not deign to pay us the slightest attention. In Patricia's eyes I saw that solemn, remote expression which had been there on the first morning I met her, when she was watching the wild animals.

"In the old days," Patricia said, in a low, husky voice, "before a *morane* could call himself a man or have the right to a wife, he had to kill a lion. Not from long range with a powerful gun, either. With his spear and machete."

By now the cattle were lined up ready to move out of the corral. Yet the young warriors made no move to lift away the big hurdle blocking the entrance. Then each of them went up to a cow, and made a tiny incision in its neck with the sharp filed point of his spear. Each put his mouth to the fresh wound and sucked the blood out in great gulps. Then they held one hand over the nick they had made and waited till it clotted. The cows had not so much as mooed.

"That is all the nourishment they get," Patricia said. "Milk in the evening; blood in the morning."

The thorny hurdle was now removed, and the herd streamed out to graze, with Oriunga leading them. As he passed close by us, his tongue came out and licked a streak of red off his dark cheek. His eyes, burning and contemptuous, glanced for a moment over Patricia. Then he moved on, proud as a demigod, though his only food was blood and milk, his only shelter the dung cast by his scrawny cows.

6

Patricia was silent and thoughtful. I asked her whether we might go back to the car.

"If you like," she said.

We completed our circuit of the hilltop. By now the *manyatta*, on its narrow plateau, was complete. If I had not actually seen it under construction, it is just possible I should not have noticed it. The thorny zareba blended into the natural clumps of thorn bushes dotted about the little hill. The *manyatta* itself stood scarcely higher than the prickly hedge protecting it, and was already sun-baked to the color of parched earth. It resembled a kind of giant curling caterpillar, and its brownish texture made it easily mistakable for a fold or ridge of earth in the bush.

It was then that I recollected having seen walls similar to these, on more than one occasion, crumbling away at the top of the little knolls scattered about the savannah. I had never guessed how they came to be there.

Now that the stench had evaporated, and clouds of flies were not buzzing angrily round my head, I could better appreciate the admiration which Patricia had expressed for this wattle-and-dung creation. It was a striking testament to the ingenuity of poverty, and the best possible defense the Masai could have against the only enemies they feared on this earth—the burden of stability, the putting down of roots, attachment to any one permanent home. There could have been no finer dwelling-place for these eternal nomads than the *manyatta*. It was the makeshift house *par excellence*, a temporary refuge that was easy to build, no trouble to abandon, and liable to crumble away soon after it was vacated.

Kihoro stood with his fractured pelvis propped against the side of the car, his rifle unslung, staring at the *manyatta* out of his one sound eye. Patricia said not a word to him; she hardly seemed to notice his existence.

When we had all taken our places in the car once more, it was to Patricia, not me, that Bogo turned for instructions. But Patricia either failed to observe this, or refused to let on that she had done so: so Bogo decided to drive back along the route by which we had come. Patricia lay back with her eyes shut: she seemed to be asleep. But I knew her too well by now to be taken in by this pose. While feigning apathy she was, in point of fact, thinking hard.

A short distance in front of us a moving cloud of dust showed where the Masai herd was still on the march. When we caught up with them, Bogo gave them a very wide berth in passing. On either flank of the herd, high above the swirling dust, gleamed the exotic topknot of a *morane*. In the van, haloed with clouds of dusty glory, advanced the helmet of plaited hair which belonged to Oriunga.

Patricia half-opened her eyes. I thought she was reflecting on the most handsome and savage of the three young warriors as a man; but not a bit of it. Her mind was preoccupied with the thought of the blood he had recently drunk.

She said: "When I began to feed King on raw meat, he used to wolf it down so noisily, and with such enjoyment, that I tried it too. But it wasn't very nice. Later on, Kihoro used to go outside the Reserve with his gun and kill game for King to eat. Later still King went hunting on his own account. To begin with he would bring gazelle or antelope back to the house—he carried them in his mouth, you know. But Mummy didn't like that. That was when my father had to punish King a lot—and when he tore the *kiboko* to bits after being beaten with it."

As she thought of this incident, Patricia giggled slightly. But almost at once her face fell back into those serious, almost harsh lines which aged her in so striking a fashion.

"The happiest moments of King's life," Patricia remarked, "were when he was licking the blood off his chops. Or so I thought. Anyway, I tried that too, once or twice. I soaked my finger in blood and licked it clean. It tasted horrid."

Patricia turned and looked out of the back of the car. But the herd and its leader had passed out of sight. Even the dust cloud had dwindled to a barely discernible pencil mark on the sky.

"I haven't wanted to taste blood for ages now," Patricia said. "But when that *morane* started licking the blood off his lips just now—you saw him, didn't you?—it made me think of King. Just for a second or so I felt the urge again. Silly, really."

She shook her head, and the neat fringe bobbed up and down

"The Masai," she said, "drink cows' blood almost from the minute they're weaned. They acquire the habit—just like those animals that kill in order to eat."

By now we had left the open grazing-land where the Masai had set up their *manyatta*, and were driving across country, following the easiest route for the car. We bumped through ravines between high rocky cliffs, jolted across clearings in the jungle, and skirted round the lower slopes of thickly wooded hills. Wild life was everywhere, in abundance: it seemed to multiply before our very eyes. Patricia sat with her chin resting on the edge of the car door—the window was wound down—and watched. It was astonishing how thickly the area teemed with animals, even allowing for it being a protected sanctuary.

"This is the time when they're all coming back from the water holes," Patricia said. "The females want to graze and get some exercise—" Her delicate nostrils and soft, childish mouth quivered. "And the males," she added, "are going hunting."

She gripped Bogo by the shoulder. "Drive as slowly as possible," she told him.

Then she said to me: "If a car is cruising gently along and not making much noise, the animals take no notice of it. They think it's some sort of animal itself."

"Do you understand, Bogo?" I asked the driver.

"Yes, sah. I understands."

From where I sat I could just see one side of his face: the crumpled folds and wrinkles of skin uncreased a little as he spoke. This was the nearest Bogo ever got to a smile.

"Stop talking now," Patricia whispered. Craning out of the window, she scanned the bush with concentrated attention.

We drove for a while across a bare, open plain where herd after herd of zebra galloped away at our approach. Then the car began to follow a kind of natural track that wound away round the bottom of a slight slope, heavily overgrown with scrub.

Patricia whispered to Bogo to stop. Then, very slowly and gently, she opened the car door, made a sign to me to stay where I was, and slipped out. With an almost imperceptible twist of his body, Kihoro shifted round so that his double-barreled gun covered her progress.

Without a sound she moved forward in the direction of two big, tangled clumps of bushes, with a narrow track running between them. Suddenly she froze. Kihoro's gun lifted a fraction from his knees. A great cat's head had materialized out of the bushes: an exquisitely shaped head, drawn in delicate, fluid lines, its light skin all dappled with tawny patches. But the open jaws revealed a terrible set of fangs, and a murderous growl rumbled deep in the beast's throat.

It moved into the open a little. Its muzzle and throat were slender, and it had long narrow paws. Its neck was more rounded than a leopard's or a panther's, and its spots smaller and not so dark. It was, in fact, a full-grown cheetah. Patricia stood her ground, as motionless as if she had been a small wooden image left standing out in the bush, and stared it straight in the eyes. After a moment that seemed to me like an eternity, the great cat took a step back, and the little girl a step forward. Then they both froze once more. Finally, the cheetah retreated a little farther, and Patricia advanced accordingly. They both disappeared into the bushes.

Kihoro was responsible for Patricia's safety. I wondered

if he would follow her. But no; he left his gun lying across his knees and closed his one good eye. Clearly he knew just when Patricia's mysterious powers protected her more surely than any bullet could do.

Patricia had left the car door ajar. I pushed it wide open, got out myself, and by standing on tiptoe managed to see over the top of the bushes. There was a carcass lying there. In shape and size it resembled a very young foal: it had a white skin lined with black stripes. Two cats with cream-colored bodies, dusted all over with what looked like brown confetti, were playing near by. They were the most magnificent and graceful creatures imaginable; they moved like quicksilver, chasing each other round, butting, flicking out with their paws, somersaulting over and over.

Occasionally the cheetah cubs stopped playing to gnaw a quick mouthful from the carcass of the little zebra.

Patricia and the big cheetah were out of sight in the bushes. What was passing between them? How, and what, could they communicate to each other?

When at last Patricia returned I said: "Why don't you keep a couple of these creatures as pets? I'm told they can be made wonderfully tame."

The child stared at me in astonishment and disdain.

"*Cheetahs?* After King?" She paused, and then repeated King's name, more gently this time. A fierce, almost savage determination hardened her features. I could not guess what it meant, but it frightened me.

"Let's go back," I said. "You got me out of bed before daybreak. Besides, after all those flies, and that cow dung, I feel I need a bath."

"You can go back if you like," Patricia said. "But I'm staying."

I had no alternative but to stay with her.

She bent down now and whispered something in Kihoro's ear. The old, scarred tracker shook his head firmly. It was the first time I had ever seen him refuse her anything. Patricia insisted. Her speech grew faster, more emphatic. Finally Kihoro bowed his head in acquiescence. If she had dealt with him as she had dealt with me, what could he do but give in?

And what could Bogo do but follow the directions and signs by which the old man indicated the new route we were to follow—the route laid down by Patricia?

I am pretty sure that very few men, either white or black, had ever ventured where Kihoro now took us. Our only predecessor was Bullit, who had taken his Land Rover into the farthest recesses of this vast, wild territory, where the beasts held undisputed sovereignty.

We passed through deep glens and thickets, which gave way in turn to dry, crackling scrub. Rolling savannah shimmered away toward mysterious forests on the horizon; from time to time we caught a glimpse of the summit of Kilimanjaro. Heavy, thorny branches whipped and scraped against the sides of the car. But all the time we were continually reminded of the presence of wild life, of animals at ease in their natural habitat. Eyes, ears, and nose alike bore witness to their activities. We saw them scattering away from us—at a gallop, or in quick, graceful bounds, according to species. The air was full of their calls: they neighed, howled, roared, and trumpeted all around us. For every beast, small or large, timid or predatory, it was now feeding-time.

Kihoro signaled to Bogo to stop. We pulled up between two thick clumps of tangled trees and bushes which concealed us completely. Kihoro, Patricia, and I all got out of the car. Bogo was sweating with fright: even the drops of perspiration that ran down his face looked gray. I felt very sorry for him, and said, lingering a little behind the others: "There's nothing to be afraid of. Remember what the little white girl said."

"I will try, sah," said Bogo, humbly.

Patricia and Kihoro had only a few seconds' start on me; but they moved from cover to cover so nimbly, and with such silent speed, that neither sound nor shadow showed which way they had gone. They were quite close at hand, and yet as remote and inaccessible as if they had been miles off. How on earth was I to find them in this thorny labyrinth? Luckily for me, Patricia—irritated no doubt by the noise I made as I crashed through the tangled undergrowth—gave a low whistle to let me know where she was. I found her crouchng in the lee of a big thorn bush. She was alone.

"Where's Kihoro?" I whispered.

Patricia pointed through the interlacing branches. I looked, and saw a long, gently sloping grassy expanse, dotted with clumps of trees.

"What's he doing there?"

In that flat, toneless whisper of hers Patricia said: "He knows exactly where all the beasts have their hunting-grounds. So you see—"

She broke off abruptly as a long, drawn-out call rose on the still air: an extraordinary sound, somewhere between an animal howl and a savage's war-cry. It seemed to go on forever. I made a movement to stand up and look, but Patricia held me back. The call stopped, started again, was cut off short. Then the long note swelled out once more.

"Look through here," Patricia whispered.

I bent down and peered between two branches. Their thorns scratched my hands and face: it did not matter. I saw Kihoro, saw him clearly, leaning against a lonely acacia tree in the middle of the open ground before me; saw, too, the great lion bounding toward him, mane flying in the wind. It was King.

When he reached the tree, King reared up on his hind legs and placed his forepaws on the shoulders of the man who had called to him.

"Kihoro found King when he was a tiny, abandoned cub," Patricia said. "Kihoro saved his life. King has never forgotten that."

Kihoro hugged the lion's great head against his own old, scarred face. Then he took King by the mane and led him toward the thicket where we lay concealed.

King sniffed at me, and recognized my scent. Then, without making a sound, he greeted Patricia.

She said: "It's the time of day when he goes hunting."

I did not ask for any explanations. Everything now seemed not only possible but natural, a matter of course. I had crossed the great dividing frontier, and stepped into the world of Patricia and Kihoro—and King.

The old tracker now left us. Patricia kept King close by her side, one hand gripping his mane. And I sensed, by some unanalyzable instinct, just what was about to happen. Kihoro had formerly been one of the best beaters in East Africa. Now he was going to demonstrate his ancient skill once more—but not, this time, for the benefit of a white hunter, or, indeed, of any human being.

We waited a long time. But when the climax came, it was all over in a flash.

A shrill, ululating cry rang out, quickly followed by another and yet another. They seemed to come from all quarters of the compass simultaneously, and to fill the whole sky with their sharp clamor. A troop of buffalo, which had been grazing at the far end of the plain, scattered in terror. Behind one of them Kihoro appeared, driving it toward our hiding-place with more of those wild, unnerving yells of his. The buffalo skirted the edge of the thicket, grunting heavily, its nostrils scummy with foam, hooves thudding on the ground. Then Patricia let go of King's mane, and uttered that soft, whistling hiss that I remembered so vividly—and which, indeed, had all but set the huge lion onto me. King sprang clear of the bushes at a single bound. And then I saw, in real life, the picture I had first encountered in one of my reading primers, and which had haunted my whole childhood: a buffalo tearing along at a frenzied gallop with a lion straddling its back, and the lion's claws raking deep into those great humped shoulders.

After this fabulous pair of beasts had vanished among the bushes in a great cloud of dust, and Kihoro had rejoined us, Patricia still stood staring at the spot where the buffalo had disappeared, with King clinging fiercely to its back. There was no specific physical resemblance between Patricia's face and that of her father. But how she reminded me of him at this moment! To put it more exactly, what I saw now on her smooth, childish face was the same tortured, passionate expression Bullit had displayed while recalling the old days, when he had killed without mercy or respite.

Suddenly Patricia put one ear to the ground, and listened for a moment.

"All over now," she said, and straightened up again. In my mind's eye I could see the buffalo stumble and collapse, fainting from loss of blood.

"You're so fond of animals," I said to her. "What about that buffalo? Don't you feel any compassion for him?"

The child stared at me in some astonishment and said: "But lions have to eat to live, don't they?"

I thought of the cheetah's cubs, tearing at the carcass of the baby zebra.

"That's true," I said. "And King must have a family, too."

Instantaneously Patricia went white and rigid. Her mouth quivered pitiably; I thought she was going to cry. But she got herself under control again; her expression, when she met my eyes once more, was quite inscrutable.

"Very likely," she said.

We walked back to the car in silence.

7

I had a scalding hot bath when I got home, and stewed in it for so long that Bullit found me lying there, half asleep.

"Ah ha!" he exclaimed. "All the perfumes of the *manyatta*, I presume?" His childish ogre's laugh boomed out, filling the whole bungalow. Then he said: "When you move on to—h'r'm—*interior* disinfection, I don't mind joining you."

We were still on our first whisky when angry voices made themselves heard in the scrub, quite close by.

Bullit cocked an ear. "Wakamba, I fancy," he said.

A dozen natives, clad in ragged cotton garments, barefooted and armed with spears and machetes, emerged from cover and approached the veranda steps, escorted by several rangers. Bullit walked over to the top of the steps himself, and the Wakamba shouted and waved their weapons.

"Complete savages," Bullit said to me, grinning. "They don't even speak Swahili; and that's the only native lingo I know. I'll have to get hold of Kihoro. He belongs to their tribe."

At this moment Kihoro appeared in front of the bungalow, as though by magic, and began to harangue Bullit with such vehemence that the blood rushed to his blind eye, flecking it an angry red.

"Never any peace and quiet in this damned Reserve," Bullit grumbled. "Now they're accusing the Masai of lifting their cattle. Kihoro backs them up. I'll have to go over there right away. If I don't, they'll go on their own. And in that case—"

Bullit raised his arms above his head in mock despair—they nearly touched the veranda roof—and let them drop to his sides again. Then he emptied his glass and said: "Like to come with me? It won't be a long job."

Six of us piled into the Land Rover. The most venerable Wakamba elder and two rangers got in the back, and I squeezed in front between Bullit and Kihoro. Only the rangers carried guns; Bullit had forbidden Kihoro to take his.

"He'd slaughter all the Masai, and enjoy it," the big, jolly, red-headed Warden said, and roared with laughter.

Bullit drove very fast and skillfully, going straight for his objective without any detours. His Land Rover, with its four-wheel transmission and specially strengthened chassis, could overcome hazards entirely beyond the powers of my own car. We came in sight of the *manyatta* long before I imagined it possible.

"Nice quick trip, like I told you," Bullit said, jumping out. "It won't take any time to settle this business, either. I will say this for the Masai: they're the only natives I know of out here who are too proud to tell a lie—whatever the truth may cost them."

The tropical sun had already done its work on that strange construction that crowned the little hilltop. Both walls and roof had dried out. Even the stink had become more or less bearable; it was as though it had been sucked up and dispersed by the heat. The *manyatta* now resembled a circular tunnel, divided up by party walls into a series of identical cells. Each cell had a single exit, flush with its wall.

It was in one of these that Bullit found old Ol'Kalu, stretched out on the floor. The efforts he had put into pounding cow dung and spreading it over the walls of the *manyatta* had re-opened one of a score of old wounds that some lion had inflicted on him nearly half a century before. But as soon as he saw the Warden of the National Park, the ancient Masai chief tottered to his feet, drawing a bloodstained cloth wrap more closely about his belly.

The action was not prompted by any subservience to Bullit, but by his own sense of dignity and self-respect.

The curving roof was so close to the ground that even a man of average height could not stand upright in the cell. Ol'Kalu and Bullit were both extremely tall; they were forced to begin their discussion—which they conducted in Swahili—bent practically double. After a few sentences they gave up and went outside.

I remained alone in the cell during this interlude, meditating on the quintessential bareness of the *manyatta* considered as a human habitation. Nowhere else could one find a similar structure so utterly denuded of all those conveniences with which man normally surrounds himself. It contained *nothing*, nothing at all: neither the most primitive hearth, nor any kind of furnishing such as a food bag or a rush mat, nor even a cooking-pot or eating-bowl. Nothing.

Outside, the Masai were crowding round Bullit and Ol'Kalu in the central area formed by the walls of the *manyatta*, and applauding their old chief's remarks. Ol'Kalu leaned heavily on his spear as he talked.

Bullit said to me: "He's coming out with us to the grazing-land. He admits that the *moranes did* lift some of the Wakamba cattle when crossing their territory—before they entered the Reserve, that is. But he's not concerned with how many or which particular beasts. That's the business of the *moranes* themselves, according to him."

We drove out quickly in Bullit's Land Rover to the grazing-grounds, where he found a miserable, half-starved herd cropping away at the parched grass and thorn bushes. Oriunga and his two companions were squatting on their haunches in the shade of a leafy dwarf acacia, keeping an eye on the cattle. Their spears were planted in the ground, within easy reach.

None of them got up as we approached. Not one of those heads of clay-daubed hair so much as looked round when the Wakamba leader, shrill with fury, pointed out two cows browsing a little way off.

Ol'Kalu asked Oriunga a question, and the *morane* shook his head nonchalantly.

"My God," exclaimed Bullit, his heavy face turning purple with rage. "My God! The impudent bastard's telling us he didn't steal those two cows. Christ, it's the first time I ever struck a Masai who was a liar."

But Oriunga, his lips curling with superior contempt, now uttered a few indolent words, which Ol'Kalu duly translated for Bullit's benefit. Bullit, hardly aware of what he did, gave a faint whistle. Then he said—and there was a queer streak of respect in his voice which offset the angry tone of his words—"The impudent bastard! He says it's not true that they took *two* cows; the fact of the matter is that they lifted *three*."

The third cow stolen from the Wakamba had been grazing out of sight behind a bush. Now it came out and joined the other two. After much shouting and threats and sarcastic insults and triumphant jeers at the expense of the Masai, Kihoro and his fellow tribesmen led off the three head of cattle. The rangers brought up the rear to protect them.

Oriunga still squatted there on his haunches, his eyes half-closed and his face set in an expression of utter indifference. But as the two Wakamba, with their cattle and escort, were about to leave the grazing-grounds for the bush, the *morane* suddenly straightened up, plucked his spear from the ground, and threw it. The uncoiling of his splendid body had been so swift, and each movement so beautifully co-ordinated, that the double-pointed metal shaft seemed to spring from the ground by itself, leap into Oriunga's hand, and be launched of its own volition. It hissed quivering through the air and struck the cow that Kihoro was leading fair and square in the neck. The cow gave one convulsive shudder and fell dead.

Oriunga's two companions now seized their own spears; but by now it was too late. The rangers had them covered with their rifles; and Ol'Kalu, his bloody bandage wrapped round his belly, placed himself between the young warriors and their target.

The old Masai chief spoke to Bullit, who nodded in agreement.

"We might as well go now," Bullit told me. "The old chap swears that if the District Commissioner awards an indemnity to the Wakamba, the Masai will be glad to pay it. He reckons it isn't a high price for saving a *morane's* self-respect."

Oriunga sank back on his haunches, smiling to himself. For some unknown reason I found myself thinking of Patricia; and—I couldn't explain this either—I decided I was glad that she had not been here to see his moment of triumph.

But that same evening, when Bullit and Sybil came round on my invitation for the usual evening drink, Patricia came with them. She waited till her father and mother were standing on the veranda steps, watching the last rays of the sun sinking behind Kilimanjaro; and then, in her toneless, secret voice—but her eyes were bright with mischief—she said: "That Masai who's such a handy shot with a spear—isn't he the *morane* who stared at me this morning?"

8

The following day Bullit at last did what he had promised to do at our first meeting: he took me round his domain himself. I would, he had told me, see things which few other people had seen before me; and he kept his word with a vengeance.

Nevertheless, when we first set out, and I took my seat in the Land Rover with Patricia, Kihoro, and two rangers, I had no great hopes that this morning's trip would produce any fresh revelations. After having trekked through the Reserve behind a small girl who knew all its wild secrets, I thought there was nothing left to find out which could really surprise me. I fancied I was becoming blasé about the place.

How utterly mistaken I was—and with what delight I learned, very quickly, the full extent of my error! To begin with, there was the Land Rover itself: innocent of roof and windows, open on all sides, exposed to wind and weather, a vehicle specially designed for maneuvering over the worst possible kind of terrain. There was the tough, authoritative, relaxed way in which Bullit drove. There was his obvious knowledge of every square inch of ground we traversed—the fruit of countless expeditions, inspections, and miscellaneous journeys, his daily labors over many years. Above all, there was Bullit himself—or rather, that basic element in him which made possible his wholehearted and total absorption in that unique profession of his choice: a profession for which his mighty body and big, leonine head seemed specially designed and predestined. I looked at his huge, square shoulders, his massive neck, bare above the open-necked shirt, and the thick lips, parted a little now by the wind that whipped back as we sped along. He was driving me into the singing morning as though we were off to conquer a new world.

At this moment everything belonged absolutely to Bullit, and he knew it, and took it for granted: the car, obedient to his every touch; the rangers, whose devotion to him was unswerving, and whose savage, childish laughter rang out whenever a violent swerve or bump threw them about like black jumping beans; and Patricia. She sat snuggled up close against her father, as though to catch something of his warmth and vigor for herself. Her small face was whipped clean by the rushing wind; again and again she pulled me by the arm, or winked knowingly, in order to make me admire the skill and audacity of those great tough hands that held the steering-wheel. And lastly, the bush, in all its manifold aspects, league upon league of plant and animal life stretched out beneath the tutelary protection of Kilimanjaro—all the bush was Bullit's, to the uttermost horizon.

From time to time Bullit would fling the Land Rover at the side of some steep hill, forcing it like a rearing horse up an incredibly steep gradient, thrusting on to the summit, where a limitless panorama unrolled far beneath us. It was like being airborne. Sometimes, again, he would plunge down into dark, overgrown, rock-cluttered gorges, for all the world like the ocean bed in their subaqueous, coralline gloom. Then, abruptly, we would burst out into the freedom and sunlight of the savannah, and see ahead of us the vaulting ribs of some great tropical forest.

Nothing, perhaps, could equal those strange secrets I had learned during my journey with Patricia. But it was just as true that I could experience nothing quite like the fantastic tour on which Bullit was now taking us. Patricia's tender years—which, incidentally, formed the basic ingredient of her queer power—combined with her obsession over King, and my own fascination with her, removed that part of the Reserve which she had shown me to the realm of mystery and legend. But Bullit stripped off the veils of mystery, opened every secret door, laid out the whole National Park at my feet in its full majestic splendor.

I quickly lost even the most elementary sense of orientation. I had no idea which way we were going, and I did not care. On through secluded patches of veld we sped, with thick jungle all around; through narrow clearings shaped like a crescent moon, past clumps of gigantic trees and scattered fields hemmed in by forest—a confused, overlapping kaleidoscope of impressions which resolved themselves finally into one rich, variegated landscape, at once wild and countrified, blending in itself elements of savagery and gentle rural peace. What had this landscape to do with such prosaic matters as the points of the compass? The morning sun shone down on this rolling sea of greenery, highlighting the bright tints, deepening the shadows, creating a fine chiaroscuro from nodding grasses and windblown foliage. All around, like submarine reefs, the summits of long-dead volcanoes thrust up toward the light, crowned with a black foam of petrified lava.

I looked in vain for any villages or small settlements. There was not one solitary hut to send its thin thread of friendly smoke up into the sky. Not a visible trace, not so much as the scent or shadow of human habitation had ever invaded this primal privacy. Since the dawn of time the only creatures to be born and die here, to hunt, mate, and make their homes in this wilderness, had been wild animals. Nothing had ever changed. The beasts, like the land itself, remained faithful to the ways of that primeval epoch. And Bullit, a huge red-headed sorcerer, conjured them all up in the magic circle of his furious driving.

Bucking and jolting, plunging down one steep slope and charging up the next, urged on at its maximum speed, the Land Rover tore round each herd, closer and closer all the time; till at last they stampeded away into the bush and vanished over the horizon, a jostling mass of furry bodies and horned heads.

Panting, ecstatic, nearly choking with sheer delight, Patricia would shout: "Look! Look! Aren't they wonderful? Just watch the speed of those zebras! See how high the antelopes can jump! And those buffaloes—charging along, straight as arrows—"

She gripped my hand, as though to instill into me something of her own absolute conviction, and said: "My father's an old friend of all these animals. They know us well—that's why we can play games with them."

Was it possible that Bullit, so harsh with anyone else who disturbed the peace of his precious beasts in the slightest degree, actually shared his daughter's ingenuous beliefs? Did he suppose that the very rigor and vigilance with which he enforced that peace gave him the right to disturb them occasionally on his own account? Or was this no more than an instinctive urge which he was quite unable to control? Whatever it was, the sport continued, getting a little rougher all the time.

Particularly I remember our encounter with the elephants. We came on a whole herd of them—forty, perhaps even fifty in all—down at the bottom of a valley, spread out round a small pool of clear water. This pool seemed to be fed by one of those miraculous springs that sometimes are to be found in the bush; and Bullit had cleared a channel for it and hollowed out a kind of shallow basin to catch its flow. Some of the elephants were browsing on the near-by slopes, pulling down bunches of leaves with their trunks. Others were wallowing about in the pool itself. The calves were playing together, frisking and butting: occasionally their mothers would siphon up a trunkful of water and squirt it all over them. The leader of the herd, a huge, solitary figure, his tusks yellowed with age, stood keeping watch over his tribe like some great granite monolith.

He did not budge an inch as he saw our car coming toward him through the trees. How could this buzzing insect, with other insects on its back, threaten or disturb his omnipotent tranquillity? But the Land Rover roared closer and closer, bouncing from hole to hole, from hillock to hillock, weaving in and out, rattling noisily between one family group and the next. The young ones took fright; and then the old bull's trunk went up and back, and the peaceful bush was shattered by a sound more shrill and resonant and terrifying than the simultaneous blast of a hundred trumpets in battle. The whole herd at once formed up round their leader, the males behind him, and the females, slightly to one side, standing protectively over their calves.

Bullit stopped the Land Rover immediately in front of the elephants. They were drawn up in a solid phalanx, shoulder to shoulder, their great backs heaving and their trunks writhing about like so many angry snakes. Bullit waited till the air was split by a chorus of angry trumpetings; waited till the whole vast mass heaved forward like a wave. Then he swung the Land Rover round and shot off at full speed down a good level track that appeared between the bushes in abrupt and—or so it seemed to me— miraculous fashion. In fact, I am sure, Bullit had found this path long ago, and very carefully cleared it.

I don't know what my face revealed after this little incident, but when Bullit and Patricia saw my expression, they exchanged conspiratorial glances. Then Bullit leaned down and whispered in the little girl's ear. Patricia nodded vigorously, and her eyes sparkled with mischief.

The car climbed back up the slope down which we had driven into the valley of the elephants, and emerged on an open plateau studded with patches of bush. Bullit drove to the edge of this expanse of dry grass and slowed down. Out in the open, the sun full upon them, there lay, side by side, what looked like three huge logs of wood with gray, wrinkled bark. What storm or tornado had been violent enough to pick them up and fling them into the very middle of this bare savannah? I put the question to Bullit. He made no reply; merely drove forward, slower and slower, in the direction of these blasted trunks, his lips a thin, concentrated line.

Suddenly something stirred at the extreme end of one

"log," and revealed itself as a head: a squarish, rough-hewn, nightmare head, its chunky lines spoiled by great wartlike protuberances, and which terminated in a massive, backward-curving horn. The other two "logs" now came to life in the same horrible fashion; and three rhinos lay there, motionless, watching the car. At this Bullit began to drive round and round the three great beasts, tightening his circle a little each time.

The first one got heavily to its feet, followed by the second and then the third. They backed together till their cruppers were touching, and each of them facing a different point of the compass. The coarse texture of their bodies, and their queerly primitive shape suggested that they had been fashioned out of great gray boulders, all seamed with cracks and hollows, heaped together in haphazard patterns during the final moments of the Creation.

The rhinos swung their horrible horned heads round, first in one direction, then another. Their small, squinting eyes, half-hidden behind heavy folds of skin, found our car, and stayed fixed on it—and us.

I heard Patricia whisper: "Don't you recognize the big one? The one with the scar on his back? I showed him to you down at the pool the other morning."

She was quite right; but I did not get the chance to think about the coincidence then. Bullit had already started circling in on this sculptured, apocalyptic group. A long, unpleasant, drawn-out hissing sound came from their vast nostrils. All the time the distance between the monsters and ourselves was lessening.

"Look at our old friend there!" Patricia exclaimed. "He's the fiercest and worst-tempered rhino I know. Look out—he's going to charge—"

And indeed, while her voice still echoed in the air, the great beast plunged forward at us.

All other emotions were driven out of my head by sheer astonishment. I would never have credited that such a huge, bulky body, supported on those squat and seemingly deformed legs, could move so suddenly and so fast. But Bullit was ready for it. His foot went down on the accelerator, and with one hand he wrenched the steering-wheel round. Even so, the rhino only just missed us: it shot past the open Land Rover like a rock from a catapult, and so close that I heard its furious hissing breath as it passed. Was I frightened? It was impossible to tell. Everything happened so quickly and abruptly. Then the two other rhinos charged as well. With their angry, lowered heads menacing us from every side, the Land Rover swerved on two wheels, dodged back on its tracks, spun round and bounced about over the rough ground. One false move, or any sign of engine failure, and we would have been done for—pierced, impaled, eviscerated by those murderous horns. But Bullit fought his *corrida* with immense panache and confidence; the rangers yelled their delight, and Patricia laughed out loud—the kind of wonderful, clear laughter you hear in a circus, rising up like a happy peal of bells from packed rows of excited children.

The animals tired quicker than the Land Rover; one after another, the three rhinos abandoned their attack. They stood together in a group, blown, their flanks heaving enormously, their short, massive legs trembling under them. But those terrible horns still pointed menacingly toward us.

"Cheerio for now, chums!" Bullit shouted.

As he drove away from the rhinos' grazing-ground, his voice and expression alike seemed far younger and more healthily relaxed than usual. His natural audacity led him to court these encounters; his skill carried him safely through them; and afterward he appeared positively refreshed. The incident, I thought, suggested some driving psychological need which grew no less exigent with the passage of time. The Warden of the National Park, no less than "Bull" Bullit, had to give rein to it; the only difference was that now, instead of a gun, he used an all-purpose vehicle.

I asked him if he never carried a gun.

Bullit said: "I don't even own one now."

I recalled that in the house of this former professional hunter neither guns nor trophies were to be seen anywhere.

"I'm not allowed to," Bullit added gently. He took one hand from the steering-wheel and stroked his daughter's cropped hair. Then Patricia stretched out her arm in an impulsive and heartfelt gesture, plunged her fingers into Bullit's thick reddish thatch—I couldn't help reflecting that she treated King's mane in precisely the same way—pulled his head close to hers, and rubbed her cheek against his. At this moment they both looked immensely happy.

The car moved on, slowly now and apparently at random. Once again the surrounding countryside became thick with antelope, zebra, ostriches, and buffalo. Several times Patricia got out of the car and went among the animals on foot. From where we sat she glimmered in the middle distance, her pale, washed-out blue overalls giving her an oddly insubstantial quality. This impression was heightened by the way she passed through these herds of wild creatures without evoking in them any trace of fear, disturbance, or even surprise.

She lingered longest in a certain hollow dell, where some underground flow of water produced lusher, greener grass, and round which grew a few trees that bore, not thorns, but tender leaves. Here there were more animals than elsewhere, and they seemed more contented. From the little knoll where Bullit had stopped the car we could observe every movement that both she and her wild companions made. Only the easy, unthinking innocence with which they accepted her could match her display of exactly similar qualities as she moved among them. Antelopes would come up and nuzzle at her shoulder. Buffaloes sniffed her up and down in an amicable fashion. One particular zebra persisted in frisking round her and showing off for her benefit. Patricia talked to them all.

"She knows the Master Words," Bullit said to me, in a low voice.

"In which language?" I asked.

"Let's see: Wakamba, Jalluo, Kipsigui, Samburu and Masai," Bullit replied. "She learned them from Kihoro and the rangers—not to mention itinerant sorcerers down in the native village."

"Do you really believe in such things?"

"I'm a white man and a Christian," Bullit said. "But there are some things I've seen—"

He shook his head. "Anyway," he said softly, "there's no doubt about it as far as the kid's concerned. She'd talk just as easily with elephants or rhinos."

Perhaps they were both right. This was a region into which my experience could not reach. But after the morning I had just spent with Bullit and Patricia, I was convinced that the child's essential power derived partly from an overwhelmingly strong inherited instinct, and partly from the lessons her father had learned during twenty years in the bush. Along with her fairy stories and lullabies she had imbibed knowledge of the lives and moods of wild animals. She had benefited from his vast experience of hunting and stalking. Almost from birth she had known the smell of jungle and savannah, and the wild beasts' lairs they contained. And from her earliest days Bullit had represented in Patricia's eyes both the great beasts who roamed the National Park and, at the same time, the man who was their master.

Bemused with pleasure, Bullit watched his slender, delicate daughter wandering unharmed among the denizens of the bush. He knew—I was convinced of this—that the gentle authority which Patricia exercised over all these animals had come to be the only way left to him (since he had renounced the hunter's trade) of still mastering and possessing that strange, untamed, and noble race of creatures with whom he had bound up his life. It was a curious transmission of authority through blood kinship.

No closer or more tender relationship could have been conceived than that which existed between Bullit and Patricia. Their natures differed radically; yet each had a complementary part to play in an alliance as natural and precious to both of them as the very air they breathed. This fact must surely explain the incident which took place very shortly afterward. When a raw, primitive need makes itself felt, it leaves nothing to mere chance.

9

No, indeed; chance played no part in this encounter.

Bullit knew very well—indeed, he had told me so himself—that King could smell the Land Rover from miles away, and would come chasing across country to greet him. And Bullit ought to be aware (since such knowledge formed part of his professional skill) just where a full-grown lion was liable to be found in the bush, spring, summer, autumn or winter.

I noticed, too, that when we reached a certain long stretch of open country, Bullit craned his neck and stared out over the windshield. Beneath those shaggy auburn brows his hunter's eyes, well used to noticing the smallest details of the landscape, were concentrating attentively on a distant thicket, which lay beyond the savannah across which we were now driving. Then he smiled, and gently nudged Patricia with one elbow. It was now I saw a speck suddenly detach itself from the thicket, and move in our direction. The speck became a blob, and the blob swelled into a great tawny lion.

"King!" Patricia cried. "Daddy, it's King! It really is!"

Bullit was smiling gently. It was in the natural order of things that this morning of perfect friendship between Patricia and himself should culminate in the most welcome surprise he could possibly have devised for her.

"When did you discover he was living up here?" Patricia asked him excitedly.

"Only yesterday. I'd had three rangers tracking him

ever since he decamped from his old haunts. Yesterday Maina, and Kipsigui—" Bullit jerked his head back toward the youngest of the native guards sitting in the back— "Maina came and brought me the news."

Bullit put his strong, heavy arm around the child's neck.

"I wanted you to be with me when we followed up his report."

"King! King!" shouted Patricia, bouncing up and down on the seat.

The great lion came bounding up at full speed, growling happily, his mane flying out behind him. Just as he was about to reach the Land Rover, however, Patricia said: "Make him run a bit longer, Daddy. As fast as he can. He looks so wonderful then."

Bullit twisted the steering-wheel round sharply, and swerved away in such a fashion that the lion was no longer in front of us, but on one flank. Then he began to drive at a speed that would strain King to the uttermost of his power and wind, yet not outdistance him altogether. King began to run after us, bounding along exactly like some gigantic dog, a nightmare hound dreamed up for the end of the world. Like a dog, too, he was yapping with excitement. The only difference was that when he yapped, the whole bush trembled.

In this fashion we drove three times in succession all around that big stretch of savannah. We could see terrified animals scuttling away into the distance on all sides; and high above us, thinking no doubt that this game of ours was a chase to the death—it certainly both looked and sounded exactly like it—the vultures had begun to gather, wings outspread against the sun.

King's pace did not slacken, nor the volume of his roaring diminish; but now his open jaws were heavily flecked with foam. Patricia sat down and laid one hand on Bullit's arm. It was as though they were both driving in unison: the car slowed down and came to a halt.

The next moment King had caught up with us. He rose erect on his hind legs, a paw on each of Bullit's shoulders; and then, panting hoarsely with exhaustion and delight, rubbed his muzzle against the face of this man who had protected him, long ago, when he was still a cub. Bullit's red hair and King's tawny mane blended into one.

"Honestly, it looks just like two lions, doesn't it?" Patricia said, in a soft whisper. But King had heard her; he stretched out one paw—it was as delicate and well-cushioned as a gigantic sponge—and placed it behind the little girl's neck. Then he drew her head close to Bullit's and with a single sweep of his tongue licked both their faces simultaneously.

This done, he slid down to the ground again, and his golden eyes scrutinized all the other passengers in the car. Each one of them was familiar to him: Kihoro, the rangers, myself. Reassured, he turned his attention back to Bullit; and Bullit, it was plain, knew exactly what the lion was waiting for.

He slowly opened the car door, swung his long legs out in a leisurely fashion, and strolled round to where King was. Then, standing four-square in front of the great beast, he said, with deliberate emphasis: "Want to see who's tougher, eh, old boy? Like we used to do in the good old days. That's it, isn't it?"

King's eyes were fixed steadily on Bullit. The left one was somewhat more narrowed than the right, a mere slit in fact; and this made it appear as though the lion was winking. Furthermore, he punctuated each of Bullit's sentences with a very gentle growl. King, it was clear, understood.

"Right, old boy," Bullit abruptly exclaimed. "Ready now!"

He sprang forward at King: the lion reared to its full height on its hind legs and wound both front paws round Bullit's neck. This time the gesture was very far from a caress. King was exerting his strength against Bullit, trying to throw him backward; and Bullit, likewise, was straining to get King off balance. Under King's tawny hide I could see the great sinews ripple and contract. On Bullit's massive neck and forearms—he was built like a prize athlete—the muscles and tendons stood out thick as ropes. Strength and balance were evenly matched; neither King nor Bullit yielded an inch. Obviously, if the lion had chosen to let himself go, or had been driven by a sudden burst of temper to throw the full power of his great chest and loins into the struggle, Bullit—for all his astounding physique—could not have held out against him for one moment. But King knew, just as surely as Bullit did, that this was a game. Moreover, just as a little while before Bullit had driven the Land Rover at the precise speed which marked the limit of King's endurance, so now the great lion exerted just enough of his terrible strength to balance Bullit's own efforts.

Then Bullit changed his tactics. He hooked his right leg round one of King's paws, and jerked sharply, shouting as he did so: "Well, what do you make of *that* trick, eh?"

Man and lion rolled over and over together in the dust. A confused struggle now took place, punctuated by growls and laughter. When the dust cleared, there was Bullit flat on his back, with King crouching on his chest. While Bullit was getting his breath back, King waited patiently; and his narrowed, half-shut eye seemed gently to mock his human adversary. Suddenly, with one heaving twist of his body, Bullit rolled over on to his stomach, drew up his knee under him, placed both hands flat on the ground, palms down, and having thus obtained a purchase, began to arch his back. Little by little, in a series of titanic heaves, he lifted the lion of Kilimanjaro clear off the ground. Paws dangling, King let Bullit do as he would.

"Bravo, Daddy! Well done!" Patricia cried, and the two rangers clapped their hands. Only Kihoro remained silent: indeed, he actually turned his back on the demonstration, and began to stare with great concentration at the wedge-shaped clump of tall trees on the edge of the bush, where King had first appeared.

Somehow Bullit seemed to have observed his preoccupation. He shook King off and rose to his feet; then, head thrown back and the sun's rays beating down on his upturned face, he began to work his shoulders about, stretching his arms and hollowing his back. Every muscle in his body must have been aching, every joint bruised and agonized: yet he was laughing out of sheer happiness. His animal strength and natural violence had at last fulfilled themselves triumphantly; and Patricia had been there to see it.

"Well done, old boy," he said to King, and shook him playfully by the mane.

"Let me have him," Patricia cried. "It's my turn now—"

She was on the point of jumping out of the car when Kihoro's black, withered hand caught her and held her back. At the same instant a loud roar filled the air, followed almost at once by another. They both came from that three-cornered clump of trees and thorn bushes which the old tracker had been studying so carefully a moment before. It was impossible, even for so inexperienced an ear as mine, to mistake their tone. These were not the cheerful, friendly growls that I had learned to recognize from my encounters with King. What I heard now was that harsh, guttural, rumbling roar which rises in the throat of some great carnivore when it is aroused to a murderous fury; a menacing sound that can make even the bravest of hearts miss a beat.

Two lionesses padded out of the undergrowth; huge beasts with superb glossy coats, their tails switching from flank to flank like great flails, their jaws snarling open as they roared again—at King. Behind them came a string of young cubs.

If I at once grasped the full significance of this tableau, it was entirely due to the expression which I saw appear on Patricia's face. Her features, ordinarily so mobile and sensitive, froze into a rigid, secretive mask. They seemed gripped, almost disfigured, by some revolting and morbid agony of the emotions. One thing, and one thing only, could make any face as ugly as this: a frantic degree of jealousy. There was, too, only one reason why Patricia should be afflicted, and afflicted so strongly, by this particular emotion. The two lionesses were King's wives, and had come to summon him back to them.

King understood this as soon as Patricia did. His eyes shifted from Bullit to Patricia, and from Patricia to the angry lionesses. He shook his mane indecisively. Patricia half-opened her mouth to speak to him, and he turned his head in her direction. If she had ordered him to stay, there is no doubt he would have stayed. But Patricia's eyes were bright with anger and hurt pride, and the words remained unspoken. So King moved away from her, back to his imperious and demanding wives. At first, as though to show us politeness, he went at a slow, dignified walk. But as the distance between us increased, so his pace quickened. Finally he broke into a run and was soon reunited with his family. They all disappeared into the bush.

Bullit got back into the driving-seat and started the car. In an awkward voice, a strained, artificial smile on his face, he said: "Well, Pat, we had some good fun there, didn't we?"

The child made no reply. Bullit turned the car to the left and made straight for the edge of the jungle.

"We'll get back as quickly as we can, now," he told me. He was talking as though his one object was to keep himself from having to think.

"Down at the farthest corner of that stretch of forest," he went on, "we can join a good track going south. I cleared it not so long ago. That takes us to the open country where you saw the *manyatta* built, and after that it's only a short hop home—to a good long tot of Scotch."

By now the edge of the bush was well behind us, and Bullit uttered a deep sigh of relief. But just as he was about to turn off down the track he had described, Patricia grasped his wrist and told him to stop. Bullit stared at her uncomprehendingly.

"*Stop*, I tell you! Or I'll jump out of the car anyway, while it's still moving."

Patricia was struggling to control her voice; but there

was a hysterical note in it that made me shiver. It reminded me of Sybil just before one of her *crises de nerfs*.

Bullit did as she ordered. She was out of the car and on the ground in a flash, without even bothering to open the door. Bullit made as though to follow her.

"No," Patricia said, in the same strained voice. "I don't want anyone with me. I don't need anyone to protect me in this Reserve."

Her hot, feverish eyes met mine. Then she added, as though only half aware of what she was saying: "Oh, you —yes, you can come if you like." It was impossible to tell from her voice whether this offer was prompted by contemptuous indifference or a genuine, if vague, feeling of friendliness.

"Please go with her," Bullit whispered.

I got out of the car. Patricia told her father to leave us; and Bullit at once put the Land Rover into gear and drove off.

Patricia plunged into the thorny undergrowth. Before I set off after her I glanced back just long enough to see a black and crippled body slip noiselessly from the car and at once flatten itself on the ground.

Here the trees grew thickly, and the gaps between their trunks were filled with spiky bushes which held up Patricia's progress. This secretly delighted me; it meant that Kihoro would have time to catch up on our tracks, a comforting if invisible shadow.

But now Patricia broke out of the jungle and moved rapidly along its verge. When we came within sight of the wedge-shaped thicket that concealed King's family den, she said to me: "Go back among the trees. Lions won't attack anyone in thick forest—or if they do, they're very clumsy about it. Quickly now. I want to be left in peace."

Patricia began to run through the brushwood, and never stopped till she was out on the open plain. The sun shone full on her face as she stood staring at the thicket. Then she cupped her hand to her mouth like a trumpet and uttered the same extraordinary cry that I had heard Kihoro use to summon King.

Two short, sharp roars came from the thicket, and then both the lionesses burst out through the bushes, hair bristling and jaws wide open. A single bound could— would—carry them to Patricia's side. What was Kihoro doing? Why was he still waiting?

But then came another, deeper roar, so powerful that it obliterated every other sound within earshot. With one enormous bound King cleared the bushes and placed himself exactly where he had intended: between his infuriated wives and Patricia.

The bigger of the two lionesses (who was also both stronger and handsomer than her companion) now sprang to one side in an attempt to turn King's flank. King leaped forward and sent her sprawling back. She instantly returned to the attack. Once again King barred her path; and this time his great paw, with all claws bared, raked down across the big lioness's neck, ripping through skin and flesh. Blood spurted out on the tawny hide, and the wounded beast retreated, howling with pain and humiliation. King pressed her back farther still, growling horribly, till, step by step, she was forced into the shelter of the bushes again. The other lioness had already gone to ground there.

Once again that strangely modulated call rose through

the burning air of the savannah. King now turned back toward Patricia. She had not moved.

She was trembling a little: I saw this when she raised one hand and placed it on King's head, in the space between his great golden eyes. Then the trembling ceased, and the little girl's fingers moved gently to and fro over the lion's skin. King now lay down, and Patricia curled up in the hollow formed by his belly and paws. She put out a finger and touched the paw that still bore traces of fresh blood, and her eyes blazed defiance at the thorny barrier behind which King's wives lay, moaning softly to themselves, beaten and ashamed.

Then even these hoarse complaints died away: the lionesses had resigned themselves to their lot. Once again a crushing noonday silence reigned over the savannah.

I am quite certain that without the sudden return of that extraordinary and absolute stillness, I would never have noticed the sound that now put me on the alert. It was very faint, barely perceptible, a tiny rasp of metal against a tree trunk. I stooped between the bushes to see where this odd little noise came from. In the refracted half-light that filtered through the undergrowth I suddenly caught the iridescent gleam of an iron spear. Its point was propped against the trunk of a big tree; and beside it I saw what looked like a copper-colored helmet. It was, in fact, the dressed hair of Oriunga, the *morane.*

He was watching Patricia. His fierce, proud face was so still that he might have been carved out of black marble. At this instant he was conscious of nothing except the small white girl asleep there between the paws of a lion. His spear had dropped from his hand. He took no trouble to conceal himself; he clearly did not care if he was seen or not.

Patricia slept on, her head pillowed by King's body.

10

The afternoon was nearly over by the time we got back.

"Cheer up," Patricia said gaily, "we're almost there now." And indeed, as she spoke I caught sight of the only group of trees in the Reserve which I could be sure of identifying—those in whose shade stood some of the flimsy buildings constructed for human habitation. It was high time, too, that I returned to the amenities of civilization. Both my muscles and nerves had come to the end of their tether. The journey back from King's new home had taken nearly four hours—an endless march through thorny jungle, through the dust and heat of the day. Yet Patricia had done it without any visible strain. Sometimes she would race on ahead, singing at the top of her voice; sometimes she would hold my hand as though to spur me on to fresh efforts. Her friendship with me had moved on to a deeper level of truth: in a way its very substance had been transformed. I had been a witness—the only witness, as she supposed—of her triumphant revenge.

At regular intervals she would repeat, always in the same exultant voice: "You saw what happened, didn't you? You saw what happened!" The rest of the time we walked on in silence, Patricia brooding over her victory, I thinking of the *morane*.

Just how and why had it happened that Oriunga came to be in exactly the right place, at exactly the right time, to catch Patricia at her unnerving and hazardous sport? Had he accidentally stumbled on King's lair while trekking across the Reserve? It was possible: the *manyatta* was not far away. Perhaps ever since then he had set himself to stalk the great beast, dreaming of those not-so-distant days when, by immemorial tradition—a tradition which had all the compelling force of a myth—every adult Masai male was under an obligation to hunt and kill his lion. What was the meaning of the way he had stared at Patricia, his eyes fixed and blazing, all the time she lay between King's paws, up to the very moment when she said good-by to him?

Patricia might well have been able to enlighten me on the subject. But she was unaware that Oriunga had seen her; and a curious fear, somewhat akin to superstitious terror, prevented me from telling her.

"Well, we've made it, anyway," Patricia said, laughing —though not unkindly—at my exhausted appearance.

We had actually reached the native village. From here the path forked off in two directions, one branch leading to Bullit's bungalow, the other (which was much shorter) to the visitors' compound where I was staying.

Patricia halted at this fork, apparently in some indecision. She bent her head slightly and began to trace geometrical patterns in the dust with the toe of her shoe. An unexpected air of timidity was visible in her expression; yet only a little while before she had fearlessly faced two angry lionesses.

"If you aren't too awfully tired," she said at last, in a low, diffident voice, "would you like to come back home with me? I should be jolly glad if you would—if you're there Mummy won't get in one of her tempers. The thing is, I'm dreadfully late."

Then Patricia raised her head, and said, brightly: "Look, I'm not asking you to do this for me. It's for her sake. When she gets cross it makes her, well, ill. You know."

Whether my influence was, in fact, as great as Patricia made it out to be, or whether Bullit had cooked up some polite fiction to excuse his daughter's absence, I do not know. Whichever it was, Sybil welcomed us in the most charming possible manner. Then she sent Patricia off to take a shower, and as soon as she was gone, said to me: "I very much want to have a private talk with you."

"It would be easier over at my bungalow."

"Excellent," said Sybil, and smiled. "I'll drop in on you one of these days."

When I reached my own bungalow, I flung myself straight down on the camp bed, and fell into an exhausted, feverish sleep. When I woke, it was quite dark. I felt worried and depressed, and hardly inclined to prolong a visit which no longer served any useful purpose. My curiosity had been gratified beyond all reasonable expectation. I knew everything there was to know about King's life and his relationship with Patricia. Indeed, the huge lion had become a familiar figure to me. Now I could and should depart with an easy mind.

But how will it all end? I suddenly asked myself, and thought: I must stay to the end. I got up and began irritably pacing up and down the veranda.

Why should there be an "end," and of what nature?

Was I waiting to see Kihoro shoot Oriunga, or the *morane* run his spear through the old tracker? Or Bullit ripped up by a rhino? Or King, the rules of the game suddenly forgotten, tearing Patricia limb from limb? Or Sybil going mad?

All these notions were at once distasteful and absurd. I was losing all sense of proportion. I ought to get out of this place as soon as I could, and put its inhabitants—both animal and human—far behind me.

But I knew I would stay in the Reserve till the end, because—though I could not explain my absolute certainty —I *knew* that an end there would be, a climax, a *dénouement* of some sort.

I lit my hurricane lamp and went in search of a bottle of whisky. Later—very much later—I had drunk enough to put me to sleep again.

A tiny velvety paw gently lifted one of my eyelids. I saw a monkey about the size of a large coconut, sitting beside my pillow, with a black silky mask on his face. It was an exact repetition of my first awakening in the Reserve: the same half-light, the same scatter of bush shirt and slacks thrown down in a heap at the end of my bed, beside the hurricane lamp—which, just as before, was still burning.

Just as I had done then, too, I now walked out onto the veranda; and there I found Cymbeline, the little gazelle whose hoofs were no bigger than dice and whose horns were like pine needles. And the same mist veiled the big clearing which led down to the mysterious pool.

Yes, everything was as it had been on that first occasion; but now the magic had lost its power over me. There was no longer any poetry or mystery about Nicholas and

Cymbeline. I knew in advance every detail and contour of the landscape before the mist revealed it. In short, my feelings were not more than the calcined ashes of that miraculous wonder I had previously experienced.

But the dawn came up again, in all its instantaneous splendor, the snows of Kilimanjaro flushed warmly crimson, like coals glowing evenly in a brazier. The mist shredded away into fairy ribbons and a sparkling powder of crushed diamonds. Down beyond the tall grasses a gleam of water appeared, and the wild animals began to weave their vast living tapestry at the foot of the great mountain.

Then all this natural beauty regained its pristine freshness in my eyes: it became new once more, as it had been on that unique morning when I first discovered it. Though Nature might monotonously repeat her miracles, indifferent to beauty, that beauty itself lost nothing of its magnificence and perfection. Once more I was torn by a desire to share the freedom and innocence which were the prerogative of all wild creatures. I felt the need no less urgently than I had on first setting foot in the Reserve: I had not truly satisfied it in any respect during my stay.

I dressed and went out, following the edge of the forest. I seemed to be moving in a kind of waking dream; I felt that everything would begin again, that all the events of that first morning were about to repeat themselves. This impression was so strong that when I reached the point at which I had to come out from the cover of the trees, I paused for a moment, listening for Patricia's voice.

And then I heard it.

She said: "You mustn't go any further. It's not allowed."

Precisely because I had been half-expecting it, this flat, toneless whisper surprised and terrified me far more than it had done on that other morning, when it had come out of the blue at me. This was too extraordinary to be a mere coincidence; it must be a hallucination produced by my own distraught mind.

But when I turned round, there stood the same small girl in gray overalls, with her bowl-shaped haircut, leaning against the same tree as before. The only difference was that this time she was laughing.

"It's plain witchcraft," I said. "First Nicholas and Cymbeline. Now you."

Patricia's silent laughter doubled in intensity. A delightful mischievous spark was dancing in her eyes.

"I thought you'd never guess," she said. "Yes, I sent them to wake you. I knew that would bring you out here."

I laughed noiselessly, as she had done. Then, together, we stood and watched the animals.

By the great pitted scar on his back, I recognized the rhinoceros that had charged our car. I reflected that the young zebra rolling his stripy flanks to and fro in the muddy grass beside the pool might well be the brother of the one that the cheetah's cubs had devoured. And as I watched the buffaloes grazing, I thought of that other buffalo who had made his last charge with King on his back, throttling the life out of him.

Many other reflections, whole sequences of related images now came into my mind. I told them all to Patricia, and she listened attentively, adding an occasional word of approval, correction, or explanation.

Suddenly she said to me, very seriously: "I was wondering just what you do with your life, in the ordinary way."

"I travel," I told her, "and observe things. It's extremely entertaining."

"I don't doubt it," Patricia said. "But is that all?"

"No. Afterward I write a book."

"What about?"

"Everything I've seen on my latest trip."

"Why?" she inquired.

"For the benefit of people who can't travel themselves."

"I see." She frowned slightly. Then she nodded toward the beasts and said: "Are you going to write about them?"

"I don't think so."

"You are quite right not to. You wouldn't know how."

"I've learned that already," I said.

"How?"

"Through you," I said.

Patricia gave me a small, friendly smile, and took my hand.

"You'd have to come back on many more visits, over a long period," she said. "Then perhaps—"

She laughed again. "I must go and talk to my friends now. Wait for me here."

She slipped away, a slim, fragile gray ghost, threading her way among the bushes and puddles and tall grasses to whisper the Master Words in the ears of the beasts that lived below Kilimanjaro. I leaned against a tree and fixed my eyes on the dawn-red snows that gleamed from the mountain peak.

After a few moments' contemplation, I lowered my gaze to see if I could spot Patricia. I made her out quite easily: she had not yet reached the vast gathering of animals. And then I nearly cried out in terror: close behind the girl a dark, slender shape was writhing swiftly through the grass. It had a flat, triangular head that gleamed in the morning sunlight. Did Patricia's spellbinding powers extend to reptiles? And could Kihoro, even if he were the best shot in the world, be sure of hitting this furtive, coiling target? I was on the verge of panicking: shouting to the old tracker, running toward Patricia, doing God knows what. But Patricia stopped near a gazelle, and slowly the black figure rose erect, and revealed itself as a handsome naked man, armed with a spear and crowned with a tall, clay-colored helmet of plaited hair.

I shouted: "Patricia! Look behind you! *Oriunga!*"

Perhaps my voice failed, or the wind was against me; but in any case Patricia didn't hear my warning. Its only effect was to scare a troop of antelope and a family of zebra that were passing close by me. And in any case it was already too late: the *morane* was at Patricia's side.

I held my breath. But nothing untoward happened; Oriunga and the small girl merely continued their walk together. Oriunga too was used to the company of wild animals; perhaps he too knew the Master Words.

The sun was a good deal higher in the sky when Patricia returned, and it was beginning to get really hot. She laughed, and asked me if I had seen the *morane*.

"Yes," I said, my throat still dry. "Well?"

"He spent the night in the bush outside our bungalow, watching to see when I went out," Patricia said.

"Why?"

"To make sure of following me and talking to me."

"What did he want?" I asked.

"To find out whether I was the big lion's daughter, or an ordinary sorcerer," Patricia said, and burst out laughing again.

"What did you say?"

"I told him to guess." She looked at me with the ghost of a wink and added: "You knew he was lurking around near King's den yesterday, didn't you? And that he saw the whole business with the lionesses?"

I admitted it.

"Why didn't you tell me earlier?" she asked.

I said nothing. Patricia winked the other eye.

"Oh, I see," she said. "You were scared of him, and didn't want to frighten me. But you're wrong, of course. He couldn't touch me. After all, I'm a white woman."

She abruptly bent double, choking with laughter: an uncomfortable business for her, since because of the animals she had to hold it back and keep silent. When she had managed to get herself under control, she added: "He asked for my hand in marriage."

"Go on. What did you say?"

"I advised him to discuss the matter with King."

I did not want to admit to myself just what the full implications of that remark might be. I merely said: "I don't understand."

"It's very simple really. I told this *morane* the exact spot where I see King every day. I also told him that he would never dare to go there unarmed." At this point Patricia shook her head gravely. "King hates natives who carry spears. He probably knows that his parents were killed by some men."

I exclaimed: "But you told me yourself that the Masai had an almost lunatic pride!"

"Well? What about it?" said the child, with a nicely calculated air of ingenuousness.

"Oriunga has no option but to turn up now."

"You think so?" Patricia said. Her voice was as innocent and demure as ever, but this time she winked both eyes, one after the other.

And Oriunga came.

We had hardly settled down under that shady tree in King's company—by now he treated me as an old friend —before the *morane* appeared from behind a clump of scrub and walked toward us. No doubt he had been spying on us for some time. He was naked except for the fold of gray cloth which he carried over one shoulder. At each step he took his whole body was exposed.

The great lion growled, deep in his throat, and his yellow eyes fixed themselves in an angry stare on Oriunga. He had taken an instantaneous dislike to this unknown native with the coppery headdress, who walked with such arrogance and stared back at him with such defiant contempt.

King turned his head to Patricia, as though asking her advice.

"Stay where you are," the child told him.

King continued to growl, but did not budge.

Oriunga came in under the shade of the spreading branches, passing so close to the lion that the edge of his fluttering wrap brushed against King's muzzle, and leaned indolently against the trunk of the tree.

Patricia got up, and so did King. But as she kept one hand on his huge neck, under the mane, the lion permitted her to lead him slowly toward the *morane*. They stopped about three paces away from him.

He stood absolutely still and looked them over. Beneath the casque of clay-plastered hair he held his head high and straight. King's great jaws opened, and his incisors gleamed. He pawed the ground with one forefoot, baring all his claws. Oriunga smiled contemptuously.

Then, just as she had done with me, Patricia set King at the *morane* and held him in at the last moment. This process she repeated several times. But on this occasion the lion was not roaring and working himself up into a blind rage simply to please a little girl, but for his own satisfaction. With every instinct he possessed he hated Oriunga. It almost looked as though the very scent of the man who stood before him, leaning against a tree trunk, epitomized the entire race of warriors who had been the lions' sworn enemies since time immemorial. Patricia had to exert every last ounce of her authority over King to keep his temper under control.

Throughout this series of abortive attacks, when King's jaws were often a bare inch away from Oriunga's throat, and the *morane* could feel the lion's hot breath on his face, not a single muscle so much as stirred on his dark young athlete's body, and his haughty features never flinched.

Perhaps Oriunga was confident in the assurance that the little white girl would protect him whatever happened; perhaps his was merely the courage of insensate pride. Or perhaps—and this seemed nearer the truth—it was something beyond either reason, courage, or pride, an unformulated yet binding allegiance to his tribal myths, to the numberless, ageless ghosts of all the *moranes* the Masai people had ever known, each one of them a lion-killer or slain by a lion himself.

I could not tear my eyes away from Oriunga. I was afraid: afraid, yet not for him. After what I had seen of Patricia's powers, I felt that in the wild beasts' domain everything was possible and permissible for her. But I now saw very clearly that beasts alone were no longer sufficient for her private game. She was feeling the need to bring men into it as well, to extend her authority simultaneously over the two mutually forbidden kingdoms.

Suddenly Oriunga raised his right arm and spoke a few words in an abrupt, uncouth fashion.

"He wants to go," Patricia said. "He refuses to be made a plaything—even for a lion."

King bristled and growled as Oriunga passed him: Patricia had to hold on to his mane with all her strength. Then the native warrior moved away, his gait springy and nonchalant as ever. When he came to the end of the shadow cast by the tree's spreading branches, he turned and spoke again.

"He says," Patricia informed me, "that next time he will bring his spear."

Long after the *morane* had vanished in the bush, the huge lion was still trembling with fury. It was not till Patricia stretched herself out between his paws, with her head resting on his breast, that he at last calmed down.

11

That same day, about the middle of the afternoon, Sybil unexpectedly appeared in my bungalow. She had, indeed, said she was going to come over for a chat with me so that we could talk alone and undisturbed; but I had imagined that she would give me some warning of her visit in advance. Even so, this flouting of the conventions caused me less surprise than her manner and appearance. She was cheerful, unruffled, and straightforward—and she had left her ghastly dark glasses behind.

I apologized for not having any tea ready to offer her. The only time I drank it was in the morning, and then it came out of a Thermos.

"I could easily get a bearer or Bogo to—" I began.

She interrupted me gaily. "You really prefer whisky at this time of day, don't you?" she said. "Well, in my case it's gin with a dash of lime."

I still had a plentiful supply of liquor and soft drinks. I set them out on the veranda table and filled our glasses.

Sybil said: "When I think of the frightful chore I inflicted on you your first evening here—simply because I just *had* to show off our china and silver!"

She gave a half sad, half ironical smile, and added: "There are times when one grasps at any straw."

I dared not look Sybil straight in the face. I was afraid of letting her see how surprising I found it that she should be so natural and lucid.

She took a long drink of gin and went on, in a lower voice: "This is really wonderful. Too good, perhaps. Too easy. You know, the only people I see in the ordinary way are a few other colonials' wives—sometimes as far afield as Nairobi. My nerves are in a pretty shaky state already."

Her eyes had become suffused with that lovely glow I had seen already. She looked at me and said, with remarkable simplicity and sincerity: "You have done us all an immense amount of good. Look at John and the child. You can see what a difference you've made to me."

Sybil's candor was infectious. "Do you honestly believe

there's any question of personal virtue about it?" I asked her. "It's very simple really; all you need is somebody to discuss things with who isn't involved in your family problems."

"That's true enough," Sybil said. "We can't talk about the really important things to each other any longer."

She looked down as she said this, her eyes on the ground. Yet she did not hesitate before unburdening herself still further: it looked as though she wanted to take advantage of some absolutely final opportunity.

She said: "It isn't because we don't love each other enough. On the contrary. It's because we love each other too much."

She raised her head and looked straight at me. Resolution and desperate courage were written in every line of her face: the resolution to see herself and her environment as they really were, whatever the cost; the courage to put whatever she saw into words.

"You must realize," she went on, "that our love is strong enough to make us suffer very deeply when we hurt each other in any way: we simply can't bear it. The result is that we all tend to transfer our guilt by picking on the other two."

Sybil's features were puckered and lined in concentration, but her tranquil self-assurance remained intact. In an easy, level voice she went on: "I say that John is a selfish brute who has no time for anything except his precious animals, and is totally indifferent to Patricia's future happiness. John says—" and here Sybil gave a very sweet and lovely smile— "oh, not often, and most tentatively, I've no doubt, but all the same he *does* say—that I'm an urban neurotic, that I don't understand a thing about the grandeur and mystery of the African bush, that through my snobbery and hysteria I'm liable to do some harm to Patricia. And Pat herself is convinced that I'd rather see her die in Nairobi than live happily here with her lion. If her father tries to make her see reason in the slightest degree, she assumes that his only motive is to back me up, and that makes her loathe us both impartially. And when poor John tries to deal tactfully with her on his own, I accuse *them* of ganging up on me."

Sybil laid her bony hands before her on the table, fingers interlaced, and clasped them together so hard that the joints cracked. Her eyes still held mine steadily, but did not, it was plain, solicit any reply.

"Life would be easier if we could even keep our unjust anger kindled indefinitely," Sybil said. "At least, I rather fancy it would. We would each feel we had right on our side, the pleasant sensation of outraged virtue. But we care for each other far too much not to see very quickly how stupid and ugly all these rows are; and then we wallow in pity instead. They're sorry for me; I'm sorry for them. I see what's happening every time; I don't suppose they catch on quite so often. It doesn't make any odds: none of us wants to be pitied."

This time her lower lip had distinctly trembled, and her voice had risen a tone. I remained silent; there was nothing I could say.

"The worst moment of all," Sybil went on doggedly, "is when you're past being torn to bits by either anger or pity, and you're just calm and clear-minded. Because when you reach that point, you realize there's not a thing you can do about it."

I could not bear to let her torture herself in this way without any protest on my part.

"You can't be absolutely certain of that," I said.

Sybil shook her head. "There's nothing to be done about it," she repeated. "Especially when you have a group of people who are too devoted to live apart from each other —and yet aren't constituted in such a way that they can lead identical lives. It's nobody's fault. Anyway, they don't realize this—yet. Patricia, thank God, is still too young. John, luckily, is too simple. When they get the slightest reprieve—as it might be your visit—they believe everything will be all right again. But I know better."

Sybil fell silent. As I stared at her haggard face and prematurely fading complexion, I experienced an emotion compounded of distress, compassion, and personal guilt. Almost as soon as I met this woman, I reflected, I made up my mind that she was vain, silly, and stubborn. Why? Because she still cherished a naïve admiration for an old school friend with good taste in clothes, and enjoyed entertaining me at a formal tea party. The most charitable feeling I had for her was a certain contemptuous pity. And all the time her agony of mind was due precisely to the keenness of her mind and her peculiarly delicate sensibilities.

Sybil was staring out of the window toward Kilimanjaro. Suddenly she exclaimed: "They think I'm blind— blind to all the beauty and poetry and savage splendor of the Reserve. *That's* the thing I can't understand about them—"

Her voice cracked, and she pressed both hands to her head.

"My God," she whispered, "if that was really true, would I suffer as I do now?"

She turned back to face me, and there was sudden passion in her voice as she said: "There's a story I want to tell you. It happened at a time when I knew nothing of the terrors that haunt me now, and against which I remain powerless. I always used to accompany John on his trips. There was nothing I enjoyed more. Well, one day we were out in that area—" she pointed toward the horizon on the eastern side of the great mountain— "on a track that led across open country, and petered out when it reached the forest. It was a very thick forest, of so dark a green that it looked almost black. You could see the peak of Kilimanjaro rising up behind it. It was here, just where bush and forest met, that we saw an elephant and a rhino, facing each other head on, horn against trunk. They had met on the forest verge, among the trees. Both were following the same track, and neither would give way to the other. John told me that this was what always happened. They're the two most powerful animals alive, you see. It was a question of pride. These two fought to the death before our very eyes, and the dark wall of greenery and the mountain peak formed a backdrop behind them. The elephant was victorious—as always, John said. In the end he heaved the rhino over on its back with one gigantic heave of his huge shoulder and trampled it to death. But his own entrails were hanging out of his belly, and John had to shoot him when it was all over. Do you know, I found myself wishing that that fight could go on forever. It summed up all the power and ferocity that the world has ever known, from the beginning to the end of time. I was no longer just any weak, fearful woman: I had become a part of what I saw—"

Sybil paused, out of breath. After a moment she said: "Could I have another gin, please?"

She drank it at one gulp and went on: "If I had not experienced this emotion myself—at its deepest level— could I have even begun to understand what the bush and the wild creatures that inhabit it mean to a man like John? And supposing I *hadn't* experienced it, don't you believe that I would somehow have argued or bullied him into living in Nairobi? He would have done that for me, you know. Poor, darling John."

The infinite quality of her love showed for an instant through those smiling eyes.

"John and I will always manage somehow," Sybil went on quickly. "That isn't what I wanted to talk to you about."

She paused again for a moment, as though gathering her strength, and then said, violently and emphatically: "But it's vital that Patricia should be taken away from this place. Really vital, believe me. Look, you can see I'm not a lunatic yet. I know what I'm saying, and I've had time to do some hard, clear thinking during this—this lull in hostilities. Whether she goes to school or a private family, to Nairobi or Europe, is of secondary importance. But the child *must* leave here, and without delay. Soon it will be too late. Oh, I'm not worrying about her education or manners. I can still take care of that side of it. It's her personal safety I'm concerned with. It's a matter of life and death, and frankly, I'm scared."

"What's worrying you in particular?" I asked. "King? The animals—"

"Oh, how the hell should I know?" Sybil snapped. "It's the whole setup here. The child's highly strung and temperamental at the best of times. The climate and environment and atmosphere of the place simply make things worse. It can't go on like this. There's bound to be real trouble sooner or later."

My thoughts turned to Oriunga. Sybil was unaware of his existence, but she at once sensed that I shared her fears. She said, firmly: "You've got Patricia's entire confidence. Do the impossible. Make her see reason."

Sybil got to her feet, and added: "I'm relying on you." Then she walked slowly down the veranda steps, back to the loneliness and love which had closed round herself, her husband, and her child, like the jaws of a trap.

It was early evening when Patricia came running over to my bungalow, her smooth sunburned cheeks flushed with pleasure. King, it appeared, had shown even greater affection to her than usual, and Patricia was convinced that this was his way of apologizing for the rudeness and hostility of his two wives.

I let Patricia prattle on till she was finished. But just as she was saying good-by I remarked: "I shall have to be leaving here soon. You know that, don't you?"

She suddenly looked very miserable. In a quiet voice she said: "I know only too well. That's just life, I suppose."

"You wouldn't like to come on a trip to France with me, would you?"

"For how long?" Patricia asked.

"Oh, long enough to visit all the big shops and the best theaters. Long enough to make some friends of your own age."

Her childish face, so trusting and affectionate only a brief instant ago, abruptly froze. She looked fierce, alien, withdrawn.

"You talk just like Mummy," she exclaimed. "Whose friend are you? Mine or hers?"

I remembered Sybil's remarks about the instinctive use of unfair accusations to stifle one's own sense of suffering. I said to Patricia: "There has never been any choice as far as I am concerned. I have always been on your side."

But she still stared angrily at me. "So you think it'd be better for me to leave here, too!" she cried.

I made no reply. Patricia's lips were white and drawn.

"I shall never leave the Reserve!" she said. "Never! If they try and make me go, I'll run away and hide in the native village or with the Masai. Or perhaps I'll go to King and make friends with his wives and look after his cubs."

I had great trouble in making my peace with Patricia. When it was finally accomplished she said, with all her old charm: "You're not a bad sort at heart. I know perfectly well why you want to take me away. You're afraid for me."

Then she shrugged her slight shoulders and added: "But heavens, what are you scared *of*?"

12

I learned the news from Bogo. The Masai patriarch Ol'Kalu was dead. The clan had just chosen an equally wise, tough old warrior as his successor. Bogo even knew his name,

◇◇◇

Wainana. He also knew that there would be a feast at the *manyatta,* that same day, to celebrate the occasion.

I thanked my driver for passing this information on to me so promptly. But Bogo still had something to say, and clearly found it embarrassing. He stood there fiddling with the large silver buttons on his uniform, while the lines and wrinkles of his old face worked desperately. I pretended to notice nothing. Finally Bogo said, his eyes fixed on the square toes of his clumsy yellowish shoes: "Sah, I knows you like to go to this feast. You always interested in these things."

"That's quite true. What of it?"

Bogo looked miserably up at me and said, in a quick, breathless rush of words: "These Masai, they go mad when they dancing. They always carry their spears, always remembering old wars they fight 'gainst us Kikuyu. Sah, would be great kindness if you go to *manyatta* all same car with Boss Warden, ask him drive you."

"I'd be glad to," I said. "But are you sure he's—"

For the first time in all our travels together, Bogo forgot himself enough to interrupt me.

"He goin', sah, he goin'," Bogo protested. "The Masai, they done invite him. Wainana and him makin' talk now, down village."

From my bungalow to the native village was a five minutes' walk at the outside; I always went there on foot. But this time Bogo insisted on driving me. He wanted, no doubt, to demonstrate his gratitude to me; but he was also anxious to make quite sure, as soon as possible, that he would not be needed for the trip to the *manyatta.*

I found Bullit deep in conversation with a slightly younger and less severe-looking Masai than Ol'Kalu. But though his general appearance was mild enough, this impression of bonhomie was belied by a pair of sharp and cunning eyes. The lobes of his ears, by a slow and patient process, had been stretched away from the cartilage and now hung down on his shoulders. He was speaking Swahili.

"I see your information is well up to date," Bullit said to me. "The bush telegraph in this Reserve functions wonderfully well, that's obvious."

I asked if he was going, and could take me with him.

"Of course I'm going—got to. Must be polite. They're kicking off about midday. We'll pick you up a little before that."

I was just finishing a cold lunch in the bungalow when Bullit came in search of me. Under the auburn thatch his face bore an expression of gleeful and childish mystery. I understood why when I saw not only Patricia in the Land Rover, but Sybil too.

"You see how much better I am these days," she said, smiling at my obvious astonishment. "I'm even getting back my taste for local color."

She lifted Patricia onto her knees so as to make room for me in the front of the vehicle, and we drove off to pick up three rangers from the village. It struck me that Sybil knew nothing as yet of the result of my discussion with Patricia.

I asked Bullit if he was taking the rangers just to be on the safe side.

"When we're the guests of the Masai?" he queried. "You must be joking."

"A guard of honor for you, then?"

"More a mark of respect to them," Bullit said. He looked

◇◇

at me over Patricia's head and added, winking both eyes in turn, exactly as she sometimes did: "It flatters their dignity."

My mind went back to our first meeting: I remembered Bullit's anger and contempt at my use of this word with reference to Bogo. Those winks were a good measure of the distance our friendship had developed since then.

"Ol'Kalu was a real aristocrat," I said.

"And he died like one," said Bullit. "Infection by cow dung of a wound made by the claws of a lion. What more could a true Masai chief desire?"

Sybil said to me: "John is one of the very few white men who have actually seen the *moranes* attack a lion."

Because his wife was among the passengers, Bullit had chosen to drive much slower than usual. And so, while open bush gave place to wooded scrub, and Kilimanjaro appeared and vanished with each fresh twist of the track, he had ample leisure to describe, for my benefit, one of those fabulous ritual combats which, till very recent times, had decimated lions and Masai alike.

One fine morning, about dawn, ten or a dozen young men would leave the *manyatta,* and make for the den of a lion which they had probably spent much time and ingenuity in tracking down earlier. Apart from their tall miters of plaited hair, shining now with the grease, herbal juices, and clay that had been worked into them, they would be naked. The only other adornments they had were the manes of lions killed by the clan elders when they had been *moranes* themselves. These they wore bound round their foreheads. The only attacking weapons they carried were spears and machetes. Their only protection was a light shield.

Thus armed, they encircled the den, creeping and gliding through the undergrowth like snakes. When the ring was close and continuous enough to make it certain that, wherever the lion broke cover, a *morane* would block his path, all the warriors sprang to their feet, yelling and whooping and beating on their leather shields with the butts of the iron-tipped spears. The lion would show himself, and a shower of spears bury themselves in his body. Then he would charge to his death.

Bullit said: "I don't know any man who, put in the place of those *moranes*, wouldn't have flinched back at least a foot, or ducked his head an inch or so. Even when you've got a heavy-caliber rifle in your hands, you tend to squeeze yourself into the smallest possible space when a lion comes at you under these circumstances."

But these *moranes* actually rushed forward to meet the charging beast, though he launched himself against them with all the fury and sheer power at his command. Their war cries were so loud and strident that not even the lion's roars could drown them. The circle drew closer and closer. In order to break out to freedom, the lion must smash one link in this fragile chain of human bone and muscle —knock it out, maul it, rip it to shreds.

The *morane* who found himself in the direct line of this murderous charge, and took the full furious shock on his shield, usually collapsed at once; yet neither jaws nor claws impaired his courage. He grappled fiercely with the lion, while all his fellow warriors swarmed in to the attack, thrusting their spears through the beast's ribs and throat, or slashing repeatedly at it with their machetes. First one *morane*, then a second, perhaps a third, would reel back with deep, cruel claw marks scored in their throats or bellies, with a shoulder blade or vertebra broken. Yet they felt no pain; their frenetic condition rendered them insensible to physical wounds, and they returned to the assault, helping their comrades all they could. There were always enough survivors to bring this mad hunt to its conclusion with the slaughter and dismemberment of the lion. This done, the visitors would return to the *manyatta*, their black skin all bedabbled with the lion's blood—and their own—and bits of the mane fluttering from their spear points.

"That's what Ol'Kalu died of," Bullit concluded. "After fifty years, too. Like an old soldier who nurses a war wound for half a century."

"Have you ever known a *morane* to venture out against a lion single-handed?" Patricia asked her father.

"I've certainly never heard of such a thing," Bullit said. "They may be crazy, but at least they leave themselves some chance of survival."

At this moment we emerged on the wide stretch of open country where the *manyatta* lay. The slight eminence on which it had been built was clearly visible in the middle distance. Bullit drove fast over this easy terrain, and we soon reached the hill crowned by that curious oval ant hill which served as a habitation for a whole Masai clan.

Then Patricia said to me: "We might as well stay here —you and me, I mean—and stroll around for a bit. There's always a lot of chatter and boring nonsense before the feast begins. It's much more fun to arrive when things are well under way."

I glanced at Sybil and Bullit, soliciting their approval.

"She's not far off the mark, at that," Sybil said with a smile.

Bullit burst out laughing and added: "Yes, she's quite an old hand at this sort of caper."

I got out of the car. Before Patricia slid down off her mother's knees she kissed her warmly. Over the top of Patricia's head Sybil's eyes sought mine. I gathered from their expression that Sybil believed I had succeeded in persuading Patricia to change her way of life. But there was no time to disillusion her, even by some sort of sign; Patricia had caught me by the hand and was dragging me away.

When she saw that the Land Rover was on its way up the gentle slope that led to the *manyatta*, Patricia said to me: "I can tell *you* the truth. I'm turning up late to give the Masai a surprise. They're dying to take a look at me, I'm pretty sure of that. You can bet anything you like that Oriunga has told them about King. They'll think I'm not coming, and then, quite unexpectedly, there I'll be. See what I mean?"

Patricia shook with silent laughter and winked at me. Then, as we skirted round the foot of the little hill, she led me on, right up to the thorny corral where the cattle were penned.

"We're nicely sheltered here," she said. "We can stretch our legs and pass the time comfortably."

I followed Patricia's example. But I lacked the natural ability she had of closing down her mind at the same time as she shut her eyes. Nor could I stand the full blaze of the tropical sun shining down on me: the ground was so baking hot that it burned my body, right through the layers of dry grass and clothing which lay between. No doubt because of this disability, I was the first to notice a most unpleasant smell in the air. It was both fetid and sweetish:

it did not emanate from the cows' enclosure, as I had first supposed, but from a screen-like group of bushes some little distance off. I remarked on it to Patricia.

"I know," she said idly. "It must be an animal's carcass somewhere."

She shut her eyes again, only to open them almost at once and sit up on one elbow. From the same clump of bushes there had come a faint moaning sound. For all its weakness, there could be no doubt it emanated from a human throat. It wavered, broke off, began once more, and then fell silent again. Patricia turned her head and stared up at the hilltop. A savage chant accompanied by rhythmic clapping now echoed out from the *manyatta*.

"They've begun the feast," Patricia said. "That's all they'll be paying any attention to. We can slip across to those bushes without any risk of being seen."

The nearer we came, the stronger the stench: there was a horrible cloying sweetness about it.

"A decaying carcass doesn't smell like that," Patricia muttered.

In fact the stink came not from a dead animal but a dying man. And the man was Ol'Kalu.

He could no longer recognize anybody: the gangrene had done its dreadful work, and it was this that produced the foul smell infesting the air of the bush. But he was still alive. Long spasms of shuddering shook his emaciated limbs, and momentarily shifted the swarms of flies that had settled on his scarred and rotting flesh. The rasping, repetitive note that heralds the death rattle burst from his throat.

"But what does this mean?" I asked in astonishment. "Everyone firmly believes he's dead."

"But he *is* dead," Patricia pointed out. "He can't *live* any more, can he?"

There was not a trace of emotion in her voice, and her big eyes stared quite tranquilly at Ol'Kalu.

"But surely," I said, "his family could have taken care of him—or at least keep him with them till the end."

"Not the Masai," Patricia said. Once again there appeared on her face that condescending expression which she assumed when compelled to explain what she considered perfectly natural and self-evident notions.

"When a man or woman dies in the *manyatta*," she told me, "his spirit stays there, and causes untold harm to the whole clan. The only remedy is to burn the *manyatta* and move on elsewhere. To avoid unnecessary trouble, the dying person is taken outside and abandoned somewhere in the bush—like this old fellow."

The child's voice betrayed neither pity nor fear. Where, I wondered, and in what way had Patricia found time and opportunity to learn the meaning of death?

"He won't even feel any more pain soon," Patricia went on. "That's when the vultures and wild dogs will begin to gather."

On the little hilltop the frenzied shouting redoubled.

"Time to go," Patricia exclaimed. "Come on!"

But as she tried to dart away I held her back by one arm.

"Wait a moment," I said. "It looks to me as if Ol'Kalu is trying to say something."

The young girl listened carefully for a moment, then shrugged.

"He just keeps repeating the same word. *Lion. Lion. Lion.*"

Then she set off, running, toward the *manyatta*, and I followed more slowly, still obsessed by Ol'Kalu's dying delirium. Through the old man's sick dreams there stalked the beast which he had killed long ago as a *morane*, and which today, fifty years afterward, was taking its revenge.

13

I did not arrive in time to observe the effects of Patricia's stratagem; but, in a manner of speaking, I was able to hear it. When I had got about halfway up the hill, the tremendous row going on in the *manyatta* suddenly stopped dead. The ensuing silence had a quality of sheer astonishment about it—an eloquent tribute by the Masai to this little white girl who had a lion under her control. Their silent homage did not last long, however; by the time I reached the thorny zareba surrounding the *manyatta*, festivities were in full swing once more, and the noise had redoubled in volume. When I got inside and could see what was going on, the total effect was overwhelming: a savage, garish kaleidoscope of sound and color and rhythmic movement. Both the setting and the performers were something out of this world.

The *manyatta* looked exactly like a long, brown, ringed caterpillar, looping back on itself: it was low and arched, and roofed over with one continuous layer of baked mud. This mud roof was surported at intervals by the overarching branches I had seen a day or so ago, all dripping with

wet cow dung. In the space enclosed by this curling caterpillar the whole clan was assembled.

All of them, with the exception of a dozen or so young
men who had a specially reserved place in the center of
the plateau, were crowded against the cracked wall of
the *manyatta,* thus forming a kind of outer circle. The
women and girls were dressed up in all their finery. They
had on cotton dresses, dyed in bright, crude colors; their
necks, wrists, and ankles were loaded with silver brace-
lets; and they wore ornaments of lava or copper. (The
material for these came from dry stream beds and the tiny
extinct volcanoes that were dotted about all over the
bush.) The older women had earlobes like long loops of
fleshy string, which hung down to their shoulders and
were weighted with pieces of wood or iron or tightly rolled
cloth. They were completely detached from the cartilage,
and the women swung them with great dignity as they
walked.

The only decorations the men carried were their spears
—with the exception, that is, of the young men, who were
circling round the center of the open space, one behind
the other. Each of these bore, in addition to his spear, a
long sword-like machete and a stout cowhide shield,
painted in glaring colors and decorated with outlandish
symbols. They all had different ornaments as well: ostrich
plumes nodding above their foreheads, or ivory earrings,
or necklaces of glass beads. But only the three *moranes,*
who led the procession, wore their hair long and dressed;
the others, who had either passed the privileged age or
not yet attained it, had their heads shaven like the rest of
the tribe. The *moranes,* too, were alone in wearing those

most coveted of all trophies in Masai eyes; the teeth, claws, or skin of a lion. And it was Oriunga, the tallest and most striking of them all, who now headed this winding procession, with the lion's royal mane a halo about his clay-daubed, plaited topknot.

All these weapons and ornaments quivered and jangled and shook in time with the rhythmic motions of their owners' dark, vigorous, youthful bodies. The drape of cloth flung over one shoulder concealed none of their physical attributes. On they went, one behind the other, round and round, moving faster the whole time and twisting their bodies into increasingly grotesque contortions.

It was neither a march nor a dance in the strict sense, so much as a circular sequence of convulsive leaps and bounds and sudden rushes that stopped almost before they had begun. There were no formal rules or patterns; each participant was his own master—or rather, adept at releasing his body into a trance-like state which appeared to dissociate every limb from any central nervous control. Every muscle and joint and ligament, each individual toe bone and finger bone behaved as though they had separate, individual existences and were all convulsed by their own private St. Vitus's dance.

The thick, hoarse, animal sounds that burst from their chests and throats, and kept time with the rhythms of their twitching limbs, could hardly be classified as either speech or chant. What emerged was a kind of endless shout, which wavered, broke off short, began again, died down, and surged up once more in delirious ecstasy. Each member of the troupe had his own version of it, modified according to personal whim. One made it sound happy, another turned it into a lament, a third gave it a plaintive, wistful note, and a fourth made a yell of triumph out of it.

Yet there *was* some indefinable kind of unity here, permeating not only these formless, uncontrolled, disordered movements, but also the voices, individual, uncadenced, which accompanied them. Through them all ran a certain wild, primitive harmony. There was no rational pattern controlling it; it came from the guts, and belonged to a side of the human make-up over which disciplined gestures and concerted rhythms had absolutely no control. It sprang from the enfevered pulsing of the blood, from man's defiance of destiny, from the mad delirium of battle and sexual passion, from what might be termed a collective, tribal ecstasy.

The men and women who lined the inner wall of the *manyatta* experienced its seductive power too. They shouted and clapped their hands, acting simultaneously as orchestra, chorus, and audience. And though they remained motionless, one could feel that they were caught up and carried away by the convulsive stamping and writhing of the young warriors, and, through their mediation, delivered over to the same inner demons.

As for the young men themselves, their black, masklike faces possessed an almost funereal beauty: these stiffly carved features were like the profiles on some ancient Egyptian tomb. And the finest of them all was Oriunga. Beneath the lion's mane and the great plaited mass of coppery hair, his face conveyed a unique impression of beauty and mystery and terrifying fierceness.

When I succeeded in detaching my attention from the protagonists in the tableau (their stage *décor* the low wall of the *manyatta,* their backdrop mile upon mile of sun-drenched sky and bush) I spotted Bullit and Sybil. They were sitting on a square sheet of material like that the Masai used for their dress. Between them was Patricia, kneeling to get a better view. I wormed my way round to them from behind.

"What are they saying?" I asked Patricia.

Without moving, she whispered: "They're telling the story of Ol'Kalu's great hunt when he was young. The teeth and claws and mane belong to the lion that he killed."

"How far have they got?"

"They've just got the lion encircled," Patricia muttered, impatiently. "Now be quiet and let me listen."

Then Sybil, keeping one eye on her daughter's eager, concentrated face, leaned quietly across to me and murmured: "Well? Has she agreed to leave?"

"I couldn't do a thing with her," I said, in a low voice.

Sybil's expression did not change in the slightest degree. But, mechanically, she took her dark glasses out of a pocket, and put them on. (It is true that the sun was beating down vertically now on the open space behind the *manyatta*.) With her eyes thus carefully camouflaged, she watched Patricia with the closest attention.

Patricia was paying no attention to us whatsoever. She belonged entirely to her savage surroundings. Minute by minute the atmosphere heightened toward a climax of madness and possession. The stamping of feet that shook the ground beneath us now became quicker and quicker in tempo. The circle traced by the procession grew increasingly haphazard. Limbs trembled more intensely, bodies and buttocks shimmied with greater abandon. Knees and ankles knocked together, shoulders and bellies vibrated. But the mainspring of these unco-ordinated bodies appeared to reside in their long, black, sinuous, muscular necks. At one moment they would be sunk in on themselves, almost invisible; at the next they would dart out and up, turning and twisting like snakes. Double-jointed, seemingly invertebrate, they were involved in a ceremonial dance that might have been designed for their benefit alone. And the yelling and shouting made tendons and veins stand out on them like great creepers on a tree trunk.

The men and women ranged in front of the *manyatta* wall took up these cries, redoubled and multiplied them. Though they still did not budge from where they stood, their own necks now began to weave back and forth in a quick, even, sinuous motion.

Then abruptly all the warriors sprang into the air simultaneously, spears and swords outstretched, brandishing their shields. There came the metallic thwack of weapons being banged against thick cowhide.

I leaned over Bullit's shoulder—he was sitting in front of me—and asked if it was the end of the hunt, the death of the lion, which they were now miming. He nodded without turning his head. Then I saw that the muscles round his heavy neck were twitching, and became aware that strange forces were tugging hard at my own. Even we were affected by the frenzy of the Masai.

I looked at Patricia. She knelt there, stiff and erect, knees close together. Her face was tranquil enough, but her lips were moving rapidly. She was repeating to herself the words howled by the warriors and then repeated in chorus by the remainder of the clan.

Only Sybil, her eyes still hidden behind their smoked lenses, remained untouched by the strong magic which this collective furore generated. It was true that her cheeks and the corners of her mouth had begun to pucker and twitch, as though with some sort of nervous tic: this was a symptom I recognized. It heralded a real emotional crisis. Yet the events of the past few days had, I imagined, cured Sybil's troubles in this field. I thought of all she had told me, out there on my veranda, and of the cool, clear intelligence which had then inspired her. I thought for a moment of recalling her own words on that occasion: such a reminder might help her to get control of her nerves again. But it was plainly impossible. I could no more have spoken than she could have heard me out.

The procession of warriors was still intoning its confused, and confusing, chant. But these pants and grunts torn from sweat-streaked, heaving chests had lost all human characteristics. Spears and swords still hammered at cowhide shields. Those black necks now resembled furious writhing snakes.

Suddenly a group of little girls—two, three, up to ten in all—jumped up briskly from their places in the audience and formed a second procession. This file was an exact duplicate of that led by the tranced, hypnotic warriors; and the girls set themselves to reproduce all the gestures of this trance, from head to toe. Their stick-like limbs and narrow buttocks and skinny shoulders began to shudder and twitch and jump. They flung themselves into the whole exhausting, savage ritual that had produced so extraordinary a state of dissociation in the young men. But when the girls began to howl and shriek, foam formed at the corners of their mouths, and their eyes turned up till only the whites showed.

I felt Sybil's nails digging into my palm. She sat bolt upright and said: "I thought I could take it, but I can't. It's too revolting for words. To think that those girls are already—*married* to those crazy lunatics—" Almost in a scream she added: "Ask John if that isn't true! Go on, ask him!"

"Oh, it's true enough," Bullit said, without turning round. "But they aren't really married till they've graduated from the status of *morane,* so to speak. Up till then they merely have concubines."

Suddenly Patricia said, in clipped, harsh, barely recognizable tones: "For heaven's sake, *do* stop talking! This is the grand climax. The *moranes* have returned to the *manyatta* with their trophies from the lion."

The two parallel files were weaving in and out, opening and shutting their ranks.

"Look at Patricia," Sybil whispered. "It's *horrible.*"

Patricia was still on her knees, but her body and shoulders and neck—above all, that white and delicate young neck of hers—were beginning to shudder and heave and lose their normal co-ordination.

"John! *John!*" Sybil cried. But Bullit made no reply; at this precise moment Oriunga, with his followers crowding behind him, came over to where we sat and began to harangue Bullit, waving his spear to point each remark. Despite myself, I turned and glanced at the rangers. They were leaning on their rifles and laughing heartily.

Bullit looked questioningly at Wainana, who was standing beside him. The new chief of the clan translated the *morane's* words into Swahili. He spoke slowly and deliberately, and Sybil understood the gist of his remarks.

"John!" she gasped. *"He wants to have Patricia as his wife!"*

Bullit got lazily to his feet. He put one arm round Sybil's

shoulders and said to her, in a very gentle voice: "Don't let it worry you, darling. It isn't an insult. On the contrary, it's a great honor. Oriunga is their finest *morane*."

"What is your reply going to be?" Sybil demanded. Her lips were pale, and she found some difficulty in getting the words out.

"Oh, that Oriunga isn't a full-grown man yet, and that we'll think about it later. Since they're leaving the Reserve at the end of this week—"

He turned to Wainana and spoke to him in Swahili. Wainana passed the message on to Oriunga.

Despite the horrible heat Sybil was now actually shivering. In a wavering, near-hysterical voice she said to Patricia: "Get up! Don't stay on your knees in front of a savage!"

Patricia did as she was told. Her expression remained calm, but her eyes were wary. She was clearly waiting for something else.

Oriunga gave her a long, mad stare, tore the lion's mane from his head, fixed it high on his spear point, and made what looked like a frenzied appeal to heaven. Then his neck sank on his shoulders, rose again, and sent an odd undulation running down the whole length of his spinal column. His limbs went soft, as though they had been filleted; his pelvis might have been broken to look at him, and all his joints dislocated. He set off round the circle once more, the other warriors behind him, all twisting their bodies to the same rhythm as before. Beside them the little girls went through the same evolutions and under went similar convulsions: their lips were still flecked with foam, and their eyeballs still inverted.

Patricia made a movement as if to join them. Sybil held on to her hard, with both hands.

"For God's sake, John," she said. "Let's get out of here right away, or I'll be sick."

Bullit said: "All right, darling, you go. I've got to stay a little longer. It would be a frightful insult if I didn't. You've got to look at it from their point of view. They have their dignity, after all."

This time there was not a trace of irony or malicious implication in his use of the word.

"Please go back with Sybil and Pat," he said to me. "A ranger can drive you, and bring the Land Rover back for me afterward."

When we had left the *manyatta* far behind us we could still hear the uproar going on. This merely served to accentuate the silence in the car. To break it I asked Patricia whether the festivities would go on for long.

"All day and all night," Patricia said.

Sybil had her daughter on her knees again. She was breathing deeply, as though she had just recovered from a fainting fit. She bent down over Patricia's smooth cropped head and said: "What was the *morane* shouting about, right at the end?"

"I couldn't make that bit out, Mummy," Patricia said sweetly. "Anyway, it doesn't matter, does it?"

I was certain she was lying; and I believe I knew the reason.

14

I had to wait till the following day before I saw Patricia again; and the morning was nearly over before she turned up at my bungalow. This time she did not bring either the gazelle or the little monkey with her. Yet she did not come from the direction of the water hole, and had not been out among the animals. There was not so much as a speck of mud or damp clay on her small bush shoes; and the washed-out pastel-blue overalls she was wearing remained innocent of stains or creases.

"I stayed at home with Mummy all morning," she said immediately, as though she felt the need to apologize for having neglected me. "We got through a lot of work, and talked everything over. She's all right now. Quite all right."

Patricia's face was the epitome of tranquillity and sweet childishness. She gave me her most affectionately mischievous smile and said: "Mummy's given me permission to have lunch with you."

"That's wonderful. I'm afraid I've only got cold food, though."

"I reckoned you would," she said. "Good. That means we can eat more quickly."

"You're in a hurry, then, are you?" I inquired. But she did not answer my question. Instead she said: "Let me get it ready for you. Just show me where your stores are."

In the kitchen we found some cans of biscuits, some sardines and corned beef, a hunk of hard cheese, and some butter. Patricia, eyebrows knitted in concentration and tongue protruding slightly, sorted out all this food into platefuls, sprinkled the result with salt, mustard, and pepper, and carried the plates out to the veranda table. Her face was happy and serious at once.

We were just finishing our meal when Bogo came in to get lunch ready for me. Kihoro was with him.

"Excellent," Patricia said. "We'll be off now."

"Where to?" I asked.

"King's tree."

"So early?"

"You never know," Patricia said. Her big dark eyes stared straight into mine. There was about them that look of innocence and mulishness which was her way of telling me it was no earthly use my asking for explanations.

We followed our usual route along the main road, and then turned off on the track that led to the spot where Patricia and King had their meeting-place. Bogo, again as usual, stopped the car shortly after the beginning of this track, and Kihoro pretended he was staying with the driver—as he always did. I had not exchanged a single word with Patricia during the journey, and this silence remained unbroken till we reached the shade of the tree itself.

King was not there.

"You see how it is," I said.

"I don't mind. It's more pleasant waiting here." She stretched herself out comfortably at the foot of the tree. "Oh, it's good here," she said, breathing deeply. "And there's a wonderful scent in the air."

I was not sure whether she was referring to the dry, harsh, slightly bitter perfume of the bush, or the scent—

beyond the range of my nostrils—that the great lion had left clinging to the grass where he had rested.

"Yes," Patricia repeated drowsily, "it's really good here."

Her patience seemed quite inexhaustible, and she was sublimely confident that it would be rewarded in the end.

A big antelope came bounding casually past, saw us behind the tree, swerved away in an enormous circle, and vanished over the horizon at top speed.

Patricia burst out laughing. "He thought we were King," she exclaimed. Then she shut her eyes and said, dreamily: "There was something about him—the size especially—that made him look rather like an animal we never see in this Reserve."

She sat up abruptly, leaning on one elbow, and went on in a lively fashion: "I never actually met this special antelope, but I've seen photos of it, and my parents talked about it a lot. It was caught alive as a very small baby by a friend of my father's, in Uganda. He gave it to Mummy as a wedding-present. I'm not sure what exact species this antelope belonged to. We used to refer to it as the Uganda Cob. Mummy took it out to a farm near Lake Naivasha, which my father had rented after his marriage. He spent a year trying to be a planter before he came to the Reserve—just to please Mummy."

Patricia's right arm was pillowing her head. Now she gave a shrug of the same shoulder and said: "Can you imagine my father as a planter where there were hippos and great apes and wild duck about the place? He spent all his time observing the hippos, having fun and games with the monkeys, and shooting the ducks. Which reminds me. Do you know what he did with the Uganda Cob? He trained that antelope as a retriever. It used to go out and pick up wounded birds from swamps and places like that:it got craftier than a gun dog after a while. You ask him about it—" Patricia's excitement abruptly evaporated, and her voice changed—"when we get back."

She lay back again, and repeated, in a whisper: "When we get back."

What vision was it she saw behind those lowered eye-lids that could so transform her childish face into this passionate, enigmatic mask? I felt, I was sure, that I knew. Yet I was afraid even to think of the idea, let alone to speak it aloud. I sat down beside Patricia. She opened her eyes, and they were gentle and innocent.

"Mummy tried to get me to go back to school again," she said. "She was so miserable, and I do love her so much. She just can't *understand*—" (I reflected, as she said this, that in fact Sybil understood all too well.) "Anyway, I promised I would, but later." She winked one eye at me. "A *very* long time later, if you see what I mean. But it made Mummy happy, and I can't think of anything I'd rather have than that."

With a vague, sweeping gesture Patricia embraced the bush, the thorny jungle, and the snowy summit of Kili-manjaro. She got up on her knees in order to have her eyes level with mine.

"Is it humanly possible to leave all that?" she demanded.

I turned my head away; I found myself agreeing with her feelings only too vehemently.

"I'm so happy here, so utterly happy," Patricia whis-pered, and there was an air of absolute conviction in the way she said it. "My father knows that only too well."

The blood suddenly flushed up into her brown cheeks. "How could I spend my whole time cooped up in some school, and never see this place?" It was a cry from the heart. "And what would *he* do without me? We get on so wonderfully together. He's stronger than anyone in the world—and he does anything I tell him."

Patricia laughed silently.

"And what about Kihoro? Do you suppose I could take him with me?" She shook her head. "Mummy spends all her time talking about the lovely toys children have in big towns. *Toys,* indeed!"

Patricia seemed to be about to repeat this derisive term for emphasis; but the words suddenly died on her lips as a tawny shape, haloed with its mane, appeared in the distance and moved through the tall grasses toward us. King was taking his time; he clearly thought he was early. Every step he took emphasized the splendid strength of his shoulders, the royal majesty of his gait. He was not looking around him; he could not even be bothered to sniff the wind. Why should he? It was not his time of day for hunting, and he had no need to worry about other animals, rather the reverse. Man, of course, was his friend—inside the Reserve.

So the great lion came on, proud and nonchalant. If his tail occasionally switched against his flank it was only to get rid of some troublesome flies.

Patricia held her breath and watched him. It was as though she were seeing him for the first time, and feared to break the spell. Sunlight gleamed back from King's golden eyes. The little girl could control herself no longer, and uttered the long, haunting call I had already heard. King's mane bristled, and the joyous roar which was his way of laughing now rolled out across the savannah. In three enormous, effortless bounds he reached us.

He licked Patricia's face, and then stretched out his big muzzle to me. As I scratched him between the eyes, it struck me, more forcibly than ever, that the one he kept half-closed, a mere slit of an eye, was giving me a friendly wink. Then King lay down on his side, and lifted up one of his front paws, so that Pat could wriggle into her usual place beside him.

But Patricia was having none of it; she ignored the gesture. Her mood, indeed her entire bearing, had suddenly taken an extremely odd turn. Till that moment she had been serene and tender and quite oblivious of time. But as soon as King arrived, she fell victim to a frantic, gnawing impatience tinged with plain fury.

She darted out from the cover of the tree and scanned the bush in every direction, shading her eyes with one hand. Then she came back and squatted down on her heels between me and the lion. After a moment she got up and sat down again. I tried to say something, but she motioned to me to keep quiet.

King lay there with his head resting on the grass and watched Patricia. Occasionally he would give her an affectionate sort of growl. There he was, beneath their own tree, with Patricia beside him—and yet she seemed not to notice his presence! He couldn't understand it.

Very delicately he stretched out one paw and patted Patricia's shoulder. She was staring out toward the horizon: when King touched her she started with surprise and pushed his paw away. The lion quivered with pleasure: at last, it seemed, their game was beginning. He patted Patricia again, a little harder; this time she not only pushed him away, but hit him with real violence. "Keep quiet, you idiot!" she shouted savagely.

King backed away slowly, and lay down on his belly. His eyes had narrowed to mere yellow lines behind drooping lids: he looked like a sphinx. But his gaze was still fixed questioningly on Patricia. He had never known her to behave like this before. Tentatively he moved his head forward and very, very gently licked her cheek. She doubled up her fist and smashed it into his nose.

King shook his great mane once, a quick puzzled flick, and then, without uttering a sound, he got up, lowered his head, turned away from us and took a step forward as if to go.

"Oh, no, you don't!" Patricia exclaimed. "You're not going to leave me now! Not today!"

She ran up behind King, grabbed hold of his mane, and pulled as hard as she could. Then she laid her hot little cheek against the lion's nostrils, and King purred happily again, and once more curled up on his side. His eyes regained their golden clarity and tranquillity. Patricia stretched herself out at his side; but her eyes still scanned the distant edge of the scrub.

The sound of a car starting up reached us, and instinctively I got to my feet.

"Don't move," said Patricia, with some irritation. "Your half-witted black driver must have got scared of being alone all this time."

Her face puckered as she struggled with some thought that was bothering her. She muttered: "But he isn't alone, is he? He's got Kihoro with him."

I could have told her then that in fact the old tracker was hidden somewhere near us, rifle at the ready; but I had been forbidden to warn her of his presence.

A few moments passed in silence; and then, at last, there emerged from a distant clump of bushes the man whom Patricia had awaited with such fierce impatience. Ever since we had left the *manyatta* I had known he would come.

And yet I scarcely recognized the strange figure that now appeared before me: it seemed to have sprung from the dark primeval womb of time. At arm's length before him the warrior held a gigantic shield, and high above his head, and its coppery, clay-smeared tower of hair, there hung from his spear point the mane of a royal lion. Armed and adorned according to immemorial tribal custom, Oriunga the *morane* had come to face that great ordeal which brings a Masai to full manhood—and by so doing, to win Patricia. In one respect, indeed, he was more ardent and courageous than his ancestors, because he came alone.

Patricia and King sprang to their feet simultaneously. The lion had been familiar with Patricia's every scent and movement since his earliest days; and now, by the reactions of this fragile, childish body at his side, he knew that something unusual, dangerous, and hostile was approaching them. Patricia and King stood side by side, she with one hand on his mane, he with his jaws half-open, the terrible incisors exposed, and watched as the Masai warrior came nearer and nearer.

I had instinctively drawn back and flattened myself against the trunk of the tree. I am convinced this was not mere cowardice on my part; I should have no scruples about saying so if it had been. All my experience in the Reserve, all that Patricia had taught me was now culminating in this one climactic moment, and such emotions as courage or cowardice no longer had any meaning for me. This was the end of my apprenticeship; and it was, too, the end of Patricia's private game.

Suddenly the full realization of this truth struck her. Her face no longer expressed either gaiety or curiosity or amusement or anger or sadness: for the very first time I saw it wrenched into an agony of amazement at the juggernaut march of destiny. It was paralyzed by naked, childish anguish, the anguish of a small girl confronted by a situation which she could no longer arrest or control.

She screamed out something in Masai. I guessed that she was ordering, asking, pleading with Oriunga not to come any farther. But Oriunga merely shook his spear, raised his shield into the battle position, tossed the tawny skin draped about his topknot, and quickened his pace.

I looked round for Kihoro. He was somewhere within gunshot. He had to show himself, and stop this senseless tragedy. I fancied I saw the gleam of a rifle barrel between two bushes, some way away on the other side of the tract. Was it covering the *morane's* movements? Then the reflection or whatever it was disappeared. Oriunga was only a few feet from us.

A soft, blood-curdling growl vibrated in King's throat, shaking his neck and flanks. His tail began to lash like a flail: he had recognized the scent of the *morane*. It was his enemy he smelled, and this time the enemy carried a shining spear, and a great cowhide shield painted in barbaric colors, and—above all—a lion's mane.

"Gently, King," Patricia told him. "Keep calm. Listen to me. Listen to what I tell you."

Her voice no longer carried a note of command; it was

now a desperate plea. Because she was afraid, and imploring him to do something, King obeyed.

Oriunga had halted. He held his shield close against his body and uttered a strident, piercing howl that seemed to split the sky.

"*No*, King! Don't move," Patricia whispered.

And again King obeyed her.

Oriunga drew one shoulder back and raised his arm in the spear-thrower's familiar, unchanging stance. The long, sharp-pointed shaft of gleaming metal hissed through the air.

Then, just as the steel bit into King's body, at the very instant when the blood gushed out, Patricia shrieked. It was as though her own flesh had been pierced, and her blood was now spilled. Now she no longer held King in with all her physical strength and will power, as she had done hitherto: she let him go, she urged him on to the attack, she seemed to catapult him straight at the native warrior.

King rose into the air with a light, fantastically easy spring, and his full weight of shaggy, solid, furious bone and muscle fell roaring on Oriunga. The two manes—the living and the dead—mingled and became one.

The *morane* rolled over on the ground, still protected by his shield. Ignoring the vast weight crushing his body, and the punishing claws that had already begun to find their mark, he struck out at random with his sword, blindly, frantically.

Patricia now ran forward and stood close by them as they rolled over and over, locked close together in mortal combat. She did not realize that it was she herself who had longed for this consummation, who had provoked the antagonists against each other and prepared the ground with such instinctive subtlety and stubborn perseverance. She was aware of one thing only, which blotted out all else: a man had dared, had actually dared to raise his spear against King. For this attack he must pay with his life. And even the thought of this death meant less than nothing to her.

And so Patricia, nostrils dilated and mouth straining with rage, shouted at the top of her voice: "Kill him, King! Kill him! Kill him!"

Already, despite its triple layers of hide, the shield was splitting apart under the impact of those great raking claws; and now a wretched dark-skinned human caterpillar, stripped of its flimsy protective carapace, lay writhing and struggling in the very jaws of death.

I shut my eyes, but opened them again almost immediately, as the roar of an internal combustion engine drowned that of the great enraged lion. A whirling cloud of dust sprang up across the savannah, and the Land Rover shot toward us at top speed, with Bullit at the wheel. When he reached a certain thicket, a little way off from our tree, he pulled up with a squeal of tortured brakes, and got out. From somewhere Kihoro appeared beside him.

I could not hear the actual words they exchanged, or get inside their skulls to observe the working of their minds. But there are moments when a few gestures and changes of expression convey both facts and emotions in their entirety.

Bullit was unarmed, while Kihoro stood clutching his double-barreled rifle in both hands; and the Warden was clearly urging his old tracker to fire. To which Kihoro was, beyond any doubt, objecting that it was impossible to shoot the Masai while the lion remained on top of him.

This ancient, half-blind native had been Patricia's nurse and watchdog since the day she was born; he was a superb tracker, and had found King as a blind, newborn cub, and given him to the little girl to rear; and as a Wakamba he hated this *morane*, both personally and because of his being a Masai. Because of all these things, it was inconceivable to him that Bullit should be telling him to aim at any other target than Oriunga. In all honesty and justice, such a supposition could never have entered his mind.

Then Bullit tore the rifle from Kihoro's hands; yet his whole bearing betrayed the fact that he was still uncertain what his next move would be. And then he looked at the man who lay there, pinned to the ground by a murderous wild beast; and though the man was a black—that is to say, a mere nothing, a parcel of worthless flesh wrapped in a skin that was beneath all contempt—and though the black himself had chosen and pursued his present dangerous situation quite deliberately, nevertheless Bullit was pierced to his very marrow by an instinctive feeling of solidarity with him: a basic, incontestable emotion, rooted in the first dawn of human awareness. When beast and man met in combat, he had to take the man's side.

And in the same split second Bullit recalled, without knowing it, the legal and personal agreement he had made on accepting his post as Warden of this sanctuary. His duty was to protect the animals in all circumstances—except when an animal, any animal, was threatening the life of a human being. So there was no longer any choice for him. He had said it himself; as between the noblest of beasts and the most worthless of men, his obligation was toward the man.

Finally, and above all, there rose up in Bullit that primeval urge that he had stifled and suppressed for so long, and which on that account now seized him all the more fiercely: the blood lust. For years the very thought of it had been forbidden absolutely. But today he had not only the power but the duty to break the taboo. "Bull" Bullit could, and should, if only for an instant, come back to life, and know again—though it might be but once—the sheer joy of killing.

Everything happened simply and quickly. Bullit's right shoulder dipped as though of its own volition, and the rifle seemed to sight its target without human agency. Just as King was about to sink his great fangs into the *morane's* exposed neck, a bullet struck him at exactly the right point—behind one shoulder, straight to the heart. The shock of the impact threw him upward and backward, and his roar had more astonishment than anger in it. But even before the sound died away, a second shot tore into him, close beside the first. This was "Bull" Bullit's famous "safety shot," a method of giving the *coup de grace* which had made the red-headed white hunter famous throughout East Africa.

Then, suddenly, everything was quite still. Under the shade of the spreading, thorny branches lay two motionless bodies, a man and a lion, each crowned with a great leonine mane; and beside them, equally motionless, stood a little girl.

Bullit began to run toward them. I joined him halfway and blurted out: "How—did you—?"

Bullit replied without being fully aware that he was

talking at all. He said: "I've had that Masai watched ever since yesterday. One of my rangers followed him. He found your car, commandeered it, and brought me the news. It was pure luck I managed to get here in time."

Only then did Bullit realize what he was saying. I knew it because the rifle slipped from his hands, and a ghastly, agonized grimace twisted his features till he looked half-witted.

"Pure luck," he repeated. *"Pure luck."*

Slowly his face regained its normal human dimensions.

"Pat," he whispered, "Pat, my darling—"

But Patricia was staring at King.

The lion lay on his side, eyes wide open, head pillowed on the grass. He looked as though he were waiting for Patricia to come and lie down against him, as she had done so often in the past. And Patricia, who had not yet learned that even the most wonderful game must end, and the most precious creature die, Patricia now bent over King and tried to lift that big, protective paw. But the paw now was immeasurably heavy in her hands, and she let it fall again. Then she stretched out a hand toward King's great golden eyes, toward the one that always seemed to be laughing and winking at you. But the lion's blind stare had no meaning now; there was no identity to it.

Patricia pressed both hands to her head, as Sybil so often did.

"King," she screamed in a terrible voice. "King, wake up!"

A kind of glassy film was beginning to form over the lion's eyes. There was already a whole swarm of flies clustering round the dried blood that had formed about the lips of the wounds.

Bullit stretched out his huge paw and rested it on Patricia's head. She sprang away at his touch, her face a mask of loathing and horror.

"Don't touch me, don't touch me ever again," she sobbed. "It was you—*you*—"

Her eyes flickered round for an instant to the still body of King, and at once looked away.

"He loved you," she cried. "He played so wonderfully with you that last time, out in the savannah."

Patricia's voice broke suddenly. It was with such pride that she had declared, that day, how much Bullit and King looked like two lions together. Then, both were hers; now she had lost first one, then the other. Unhappy, painful tears welled from Patricia's eyes. But she did not know how to cry; and very soon they dried up, and the flow ceased. Her face was burning as though she had a high fever, and in her eyes I could see a mute appeal for help.

Bullit took a step toward his daughter, and Patricia ran to Kihoro and flung her arms round his old, crippled body. The old tracker bowed his scarred face over her in silent compassion. Bullit saw it all; and there was such dejection and humility on his face that I feared for his reason.

"Pat," he whispered, "darling Pat, I promise you Kihoro will find you another cub. I swear it. We'll get one of King's own litter—"

"And I shall rear it, and it'll become my friend, and then you—you'll shoot that one, too."

She spoke each word with merciless, calculated cruelty.

At this moment a hoarse groan came from beneath the tree: it issued from Oriunga's lacerated throat. Bullit turned the blood-soaked body over with one quick twist of his foot. The *morane* opened his eyes, saw the stricken lion, gave a victorious grin and at once lost consciousness again.

"What's to be done with him?" I asked Bullit.

"That's up to his own people," Bullit grunted. "Anyway he's done for. It makes little odds whether he dies here or outside the *manyatta*."

Patricia stared at Oriunga, lying there with his broken, splintered weapons all around him.

"At least *he* showed true bravery," she whispered. Then, suddenly, she let go of Kihoro and took a step toward Bullit.

"And what about your gun?" she said. "You promised never to carry firearms again."

"It was Kihoro's," Bullit muttered.

Patricia's feverish eyes widened at this, and her lips went white. It was in her secret, still voice that she now said: "So you were sure of finding Kihoro here, were you? Why?"

Bullit hung his head. His lips were trembling, and he was incapable of uttering a single word.

"You have always had me followed," Patricia said.

Bullit's head hung lower still.

"And he obeyed you rather than me," Patricia said. She turned away from Bullit and Kihoro as though they were insubstantial shadows, and bent down over King, her one true friend, the only one who, in his tenderness and strength, had never murdered, never deceived.

It was impossible that in a second, while she watched, he should have become blind and deaf, without movement or power of utterance.

He had no right to persist in this monstrous, unfeeling indifference. Couldn't he realize she was suffering more for him than she had ever believed was humanly possible?

Patricia gripped King's mane in both hands, with savage fury, determined to shake a laugh or at least an angry growl out of him. But the lion's head never budged. His throat gaped open inertly, and his stare was fixed and glassy. Only the great swarm of horseflies moved, buzzing round in circles above the clotted, darkening wound.

For the first time ever, I saw fear grip Patricia, the fear of the inconceivable and intolerable. She released the lion's mane and instinctively turned up her face toward the sky and sun. Huge black shapes with bald heads and outspread wings were circling over King's tree.

A faint cry burst from Patricia's lips, terrible in the revelation it expressed. There were no written words in all the world that spoke so eloquently to this little girl as the circles traced by a gathering of vultures. When they assembled in this fashion, it was for one purpose only: to scavenge from some dead animal. This was something Patricia had known from the cradle. And she had seen so many of these corpses—antelope, buffalo, zebra, elephant, and so on—that till this moment nothing could have seemed simpler or more natural to her eyes, or more in accordance with the laws of the bush. A body, a cadaver: that was that.

Even Ol'Kalu. Even Oriunga.

But not King. This thing was not possible for King. He and Patricia loved each other, needed each other. Now he lay stretched out before her in his familiar pose, at once tender, protective, and playful; yet every second he was slipping farther away from her, the essential King was withdrawing—but to where? He was gone already, since the vultures were circling nearer, nearer, eager to devour the omnipotent King of Beasts. But to what destination?

All the great basic emotions—maternal love, friendship, blood lust, jealousy, desire, the urge for power—it
was through King's mediation that Patricia had learned
them all. And now it was, once again, the great lion who
had made her aware of the reality of death.

With horror-filled eyes the child stared blindly round
for someone to help her face this enormous mystery and
horror. All she could see was a stranger, a visitor. He at
least had not had the time or opportunity to hurt her yet.

"Take me away," she moaned. "Take me away from
here, please take me away—"

I thought she was referring just to the particular spot
where we now stood. But she cried out: "I can't bear to
look at my father ever again. Or the Reserve."

I placed my hands as gently as I could on her narrow,
stiff little shoulders.

"I will do as you wish," I said to her.

Then she begged me to take her to Nairobi.

"But whereabouts in Nairobi?" I inquired, perplexed.

Patricia gave Bullit a sidelong glance, charged with hatred.

"The school where I was before," she said coldly.

I took this to be a transient fit of temper and revenge-
fulness, which would soon pass off. I was wrong.

◇◇◇

❀

15

We left for Nairobi before the moon was up that night: Patricia insisted on this. The near-hysterical passion which she had previously shown for clinging to the Reserve she now transferred—with a kind of haunted, speechless vehemence—to the business of leaving it as quickly as possible. The mere thought of spending another night there had thrown the child into such violent convulsions that both her health and reason seemed liable to be endangered, and so, of necessity, she had got her own way. We were going to spend the night in a Nairobi hotel, and the following morning I was to take her back to her former school.

Patricia had not let anyone help her pack and get ready for the journey. She herself selected her traveling-outfit: a lightweight woolen dress, a tweed jacket, and a round felt hat. She herself ironed and folded the clothes she was taking. There was nothing included that could remind her of her expeditions in the Reserve: no overalls or heavy bush shoes.

Finally a small case and a satchel containing her exercise books and school texts were placed between us on the back seat of the car, and Bogo set off, with two armed rangers sitting beside him. Their job was to escort us to the boundary of the Reserve, in case we ran into any danger *en route*. No previous visitors had ever been allowed to disturb the animals by traveling at night.

My bungalow vanished behind us, and soon we were

through the native village and out on the main road. Patricia was little more than a small blurred shadow hunched away in her corner. She kept her eyes fixed on the inside of the car, where it was dark. She never stirred a muscle; she hardly seemed to be breathing.

It was her silence more than anything else which frightened me. I had to make her break out of this intolerable state of tension and solitary withdrawal. Accordingly I asked her the first question that came into my head.

"Why did you refuse even to let your mother come with you?"

Patricia answered through clenched teeth, without moving: "She's got no reason to cry over me. This situation suits her very well."

And of course, that was quite true. Despite all Sybil's tears, and the sorrow she had experienced at the sight of Patricia's suffering, nevertheless I was sure that underneath it all she was as pleased as Punch. Her most deeply cherished plan for her daughter's welfare had at last, against all reasonable expectations, been accomplished.

"She's still got my father," Patricia went on, in a most unpleasant voice. "She'll have a wonderful time consoling him."

That was true, too. Bullit's agony of mind provided Sybil with a wonderful task: nothing could have suited her better. She at once set about it, while we watched: she looked years younger already. Bullit himself could still count on her devotion, his professional duties, and an unlimited supply of whisky.

But Patricia had nothing left at all. Was it her own fault? And if so, how? She had had a lion; she had had a *marone*. All she had wanted to do was to make them play a game which her adored father had told her about on so many occasions.

The headlights carved their way through the surrounding darkness, illuminating the texture of track and trees and undergrowth. Suddenly a kind of moving rock barred our path. Bogo jammed on his brakes; the rangers shouted something, and he switched off the headlights. The gigantic elephant, a darker mass against the surrounding night, stood there facing toward us. His trunk was swaying to and fro slowly. He seemed puzzled.

"I suppose he's a rogue male, living on his own?" I asked Patricia.

She made no reply; she did not so much as glance at the colossal creature. She was denying and rejecting the whole Reserve, with all its inhabitants.

The elephant shook itself, and crashed past us into a tall thicket of thorn bushes. We could hear the undergrowth crackling beneath his feet.

Bogo started the car again. Patricia sat there, quite still, her head bent low under its round felt hat. Suddenly she grasped the handle of the door, and half opened it, as though she were going to jump out. Her obvious and desperate effort at self-control had come to nothing; she knew we had reached the point where the path that led to King's tree branched away from the main road.

I did nothing to stop her. I was obsessed by the thought of what awaited her in Nairobi: dormitory and dining-hall, the imprisoning ambience of "good society." But Patricia, of her own free will, shut the door again and sank back farther than ever into her corner. The only difference was that she had begun to tremble violently.

I stretched out an arm across her little case, and tried to clasp her hand. She plunged it deep into the pocket of her coat.

The moon was high in the heavens when, in the very middle of the National Park, we reached a vast circular stretch of sand, smooth and shining, which had once been covered by a lake. The moonlight made it sparkle all over with glints of silver, in endless waves. This lunar mirage stretched right to the base of Kilimanjaro; and in it sported herds of wild animals, drawn by the feeling of spaciousness, by the cool air and moonlit sky. Even the most powerful and unwieldy among them, gnus, giraffes, or buffaloes, moved in a tranquil pattern about this enchanted ring. But the zebras and gazelles and impalas and bush bucks mingled at the very center of this dried-up lake in an endless, gossamer-light, insubstantial dance. They were disembodied silhouettes, drawn on the pale silvery night with fine strokes of the brush, like Chinese ink sketches. On the surface of their starry, liquid-smooth dancing-floor they glided in line, darting forward, rearing, skimming round with a speed, agility, and gracefulness that, even at their most noble and captivating, they could never equal in broad daylight. It was a wild, sacred dance, bathed in moonlight, led by moonbeams.

Patricia was trembling more and more violently, in ever quickening spasms. Now it was she who felt for my hand, and grasped it as though she were drowning.

"He is alone," she whispered. "All alone. Forever."

Her first sob was so agonizingly difficult that it seemed like a death rattle. But once the way had been cleared for them, the others followed more easily. Patricia began to weep as any small child might have wept, anywhere in the world.

And the beasts danced on.

A NOTE ABOUT THE AUTHOR

Joseph Kessel was born in 1898, on the Argentine pampa in a Jewish colony where his father was a doctor. He then lived in Russia on the Ural River until the age of ten when he settled in France.

By the time he was eighteen and had volunteered for the French Air Force, Kessel had already studied at the Sorbonne, worked as a reporter and as an actor. In 1918 the squadron he joined in Siberia took him for the first time around the world.

Between the two world wars, Kessel made a name for himself as a novelist, a widely traveled journalist, and a screen writer. During the Occupation he worked for the Resistance until he was forced to escape to England, where he continued to rally for the Free French.

The Lion, Joseph Kessel's thirtieth book, was unanimously hailed in France as his finest.

A NOTE ON THE TYPE

The text of this book was set on the Linotype in a new face called PRIMER, designed by Rudolph Ruzicka, earlier responsible for the design of *Fairfield* and *Fairfield Medium*, Linotype faces whose virtues have for some time now been accorded wide recognition.

The complete range of sizes of *Primer* was first made available in 1954, although the pilot size of 12 point was ready as early as 1951. The design of the face makes general reference to Linotype *Century* (long a serviceable type, totally lacking in manner or frills of any kind) but brilliantly corrects the characterless quality of that face.

In the designs for *Primer*, Mr. Ruzicka has once again brilliantly exemplified the truth of a statement made about him by the late W. A. Dwiggins: "His outstanding quality, as artist and person, is *sanity*. Complete esthetic equipment, all managed by good, sound judgment about ways and means, aims and purposes, utilities and 'functions'—and all this level-headed balance-mechanism added to the lively mental state that makes an artist an artist. Fortunate equipment in a disordered world . . ."

Composed by KINGSPORT PRESS, INC., Kingsport, Tennessee. Printed and bound by H. WOLFF, New York.